D1441615

THE NEW BOOK OF
OPTICAL
ILLUSIONS

Georg Rüschemeyer

FIREFLY BOOKS

A FIREFLY BOOK

Published by Firefly Books Ltd. 2015

Copyright © 2015 Peter Delius Verlag GmbH & Co KG, Berlin

First printing

Publisher Cataloging-in-Publication Data (U.S.)

Rüschemeyer, Georg.
   The new book of optical illusions / Georg Rüschemeyer.
[208] pages : color illustrations ; cm.
Includes index.
Summary: A visual collection of optical illusions accompanied by explanations.
ISBN-13: 978-1-77085-592-2 (pbk.)
1. Optical illusions. I. Title.
152.148 dc23   QP495.R873 2015

Library and Archives Canada Cataloguing in Publication

Rüschemeyer, Georg, author
   The new book of optical illusions / Georg Rüschemeyer.
Includes index.
ISBN 978-1-77085-592-2 (pbk.)
   1. Optical illusions. I. Title. II. Title: Book of optical illusions.
QP495.R882015   152.14'8   C2015-900342-3

Published in the United States by
Firefly Books (U.S.) Inc.
P.O. Box 1338, Ellicott Station
Buffalo, New York 14205

Published in Canada by
Firefly Books Ltd.
50 Staples Avenue, Unit 1
Richmond Hill, Ontario L4B 0A7

Printed in Canada

Text by Georg Rüschemeyer with contributions from Peter Delius
Translation: David Andersen, Miriam Said
Editor: Juliane von Laffert
Design: Marc Vidal
Illustrations: © Salvador Dalí, Fundació Gala-Salvador Dalí/VG Bild-Kunst, Bonn 2015. akg-images gmbh. Bridgeman Art Library Ltd. Corbis Corporation. Dreamstime. dpa Picture Alliance GmbH. Shutterstock Inc.

The publishers would like to thank all contributers for their kind permission to reproduce their artwork in this publication. For a detailed list of artists and copyright holders please refer to our website www.theknowledgepage.com

Table of Contents

Totally Mind-Bending (introduction)		7
1	Flashes from the Corner of the Eye	8
2	Rotating Snakes	14
3	Zooming In Starts the Show	24
4	Chessboard with a Bulge	28
5	Seeing Things that Are Not There	32
6	The False Bottom of Eye Vision	40
7	The More Lopsided Tower of Pisa	42
8	Locals Aren't Always Right	46
9	Creating Space	54
10	Crooked Parallels	62
11	Archimedes's Nightmare	70
12	Unequal Friends	72
13	When Perspective Is Swept under the Table	78
14	Among Giants and Dwarfs	82
15	Look Who's Hiding	84
16	Faces Everywhere	92
17	Upside Down	98
18	The Art of Tricking the Eye	102
19	Up and Down the Stairs	120
20	Impossible Triangle	128
21	Uplifting Speech	134
22	Streetlife	144
23	What Comes Afterward	148
24	Star and Stripes	160
25	Shapes out of Nowhere	164
26	Alphabetical Jumble	170
27	When Green Reads Blue	174
28	3D Visions	176
29	What's Up, What's Down?	182
30	Switching Sides	186
31	Natural Fakes	192
32	Hokus-Pokus Disappearibus	196
33	In a Color Storm	200

Totally Mind-Bending!

Optical illusions are more than merely fun diversions. They also teach us how our eyes and brains work.

Humans are known to be visual creatures. What we see, however, is not an exact representation of our environment, but rather a mental construct that our brains piece together — often made up of confused and incomplete information that appears before our eyes. In the process, we filter unimportant things out of our conscious perception and fill in the gaps to create a visual reality in which we can navigate effortlessly.

In real life, this works almost seamlessly. At times, however, we cannot trust our eyes, because they lead us to believe things that — seen objectively — cannot be. Such optical illusions are valuable instruments for studying the normal process of perception. And they are a lot of fun, too!

This book is not a scientific textbook. Rather, it is a collection of the most significant phenomena, loosely grouped together according to particular visual effects. Each phenomenon is illustrated with one or several striking examples. Main examples are indicated by red spirals and longer texts, while gray spirals and shorter texts indicate additional examples.

 Let your eye glide over the black squares and white grid. Do you see shadows where the lines of the grid intersect?

Flashes from the Corner of the Eye

Described in 1870 by German physiologist Ludimar Hermann, the grid is considered a classic example of lateral inhibition, a phenomenon that increases the contrast between light and dark in the retina. Simultaneously, receptors activated by light inhibit the sensitivity of their neighboring receptor cells. Thus, cells focusing on intersections in a Hermann grid are surrounded by more active neighbor cells (coming from four directions) than those focusing on the sections in between. Therefore, these cells experience more lateral inhibition and register less light reception to the brain. Only in the *fovea centralis*, the point of sharpest vision in the retina, are the visual receptors programmed differently. It is for this reason that the shadows disappear as soon as one tries to focus on them.

This explanation is, however, only half the story. In the distorted version of the grid (below), the effect disappears although nothing ought to have changed with the lateral inhibition. It becomes apparent that there are higher visual centers involved in this effect.

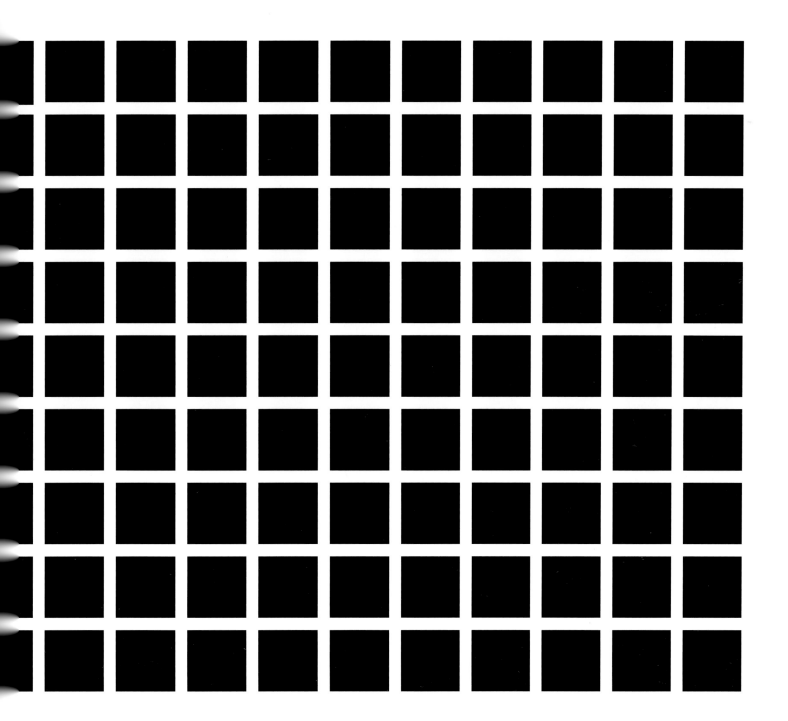

9

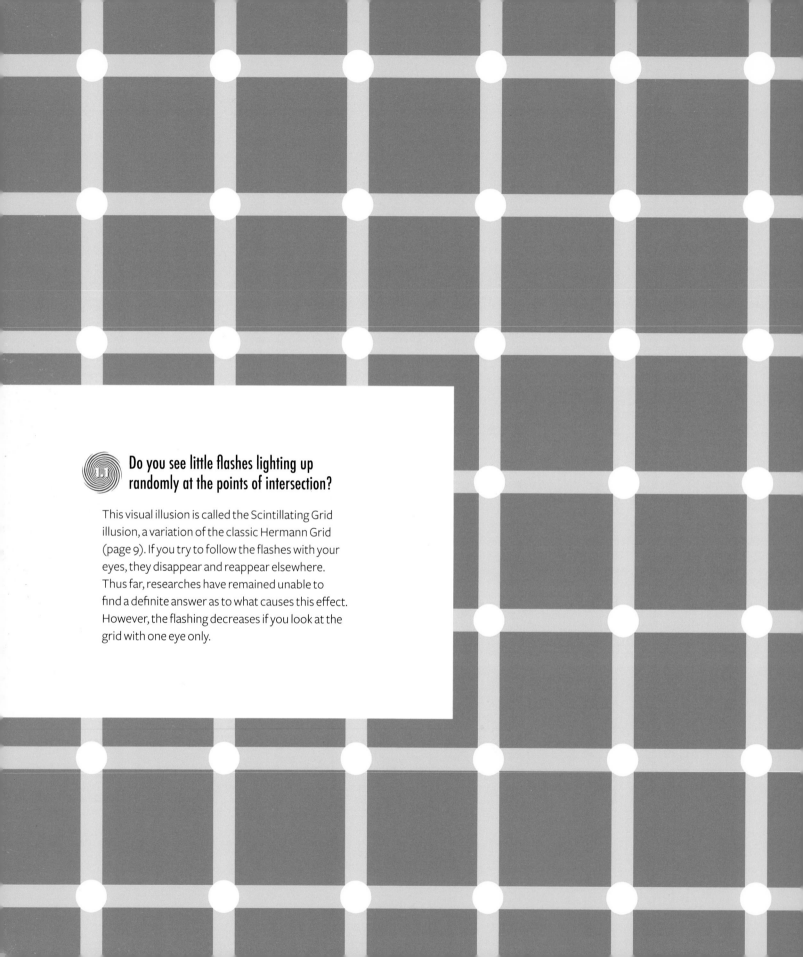

Do you see little flashes lighting up randomly at the points of intersection?

This visual illusion is called the Scintillating Grid illusion, a variation of the classic Hermann Grid (page 9). If you try to follow the flashes with your eyes, they disappear and reappear elsewhere. Thus far, researches have remained unable to find a definite answer as to what causes this effect. However, the flashing decreases if you look at the grid with one eye only.

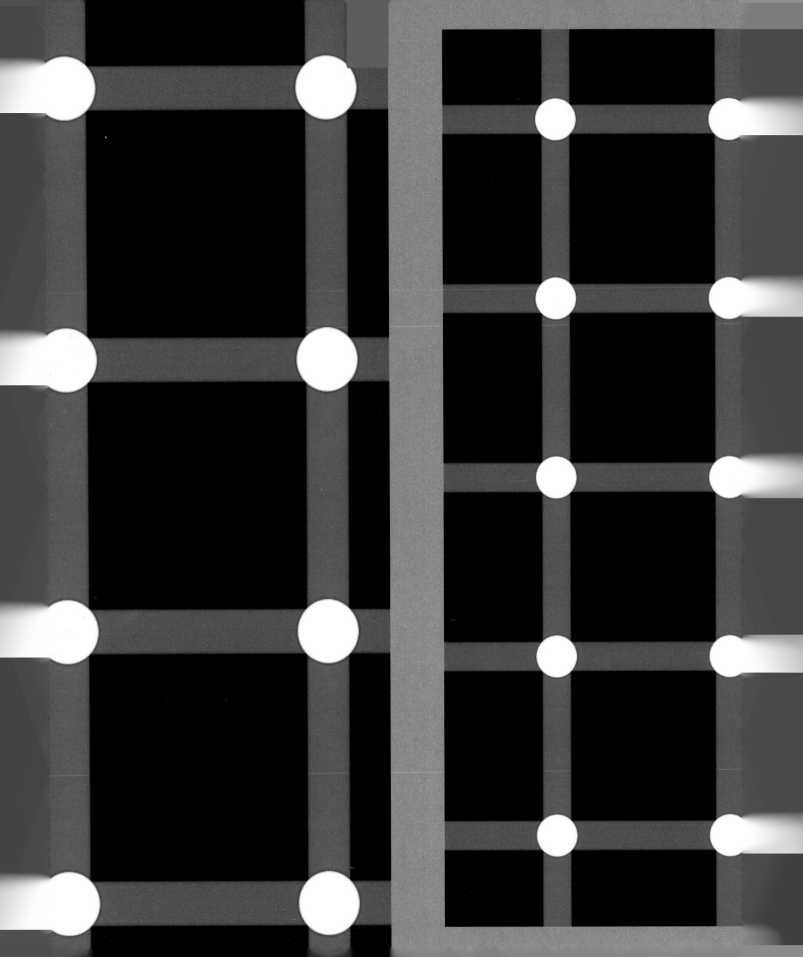

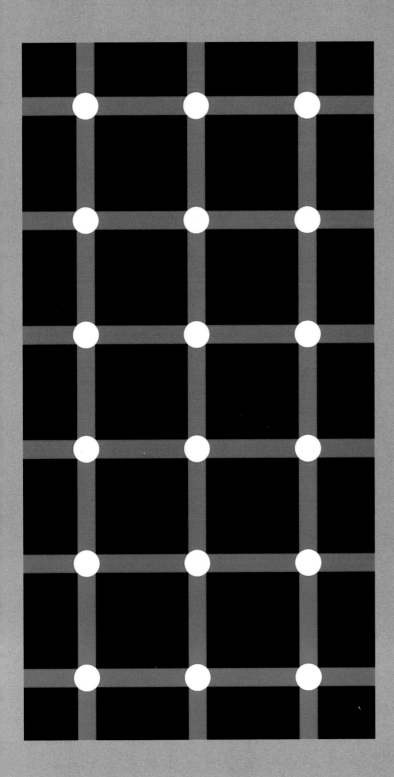

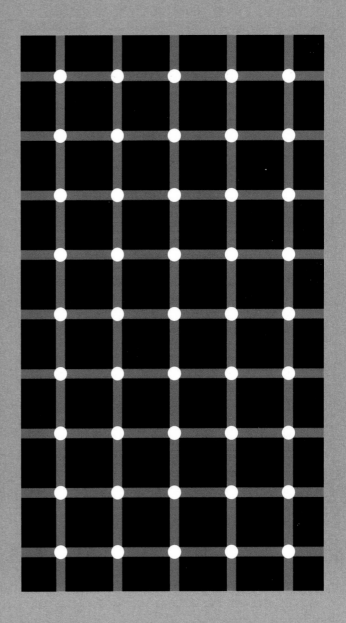

 1.2 **The smaller the grid, the more active it gets.**

Like many optical illusions, the Scintillating Grid
illusion depends, to some extent, on image size,
color, and the media in which it is represented. The
bigger the grid, the more the flickering seems to
decrease, which could be due to the fact that the
eye starts focusing on individual intersections,
rather than wandering around.

 **Look at the pattern. Do you see the wheels spinning?**

Rotating Snakes

In this impressive illusion of motion by the Japanese visual researcher Akiyoshi Kitaoka, the sequence of the varying bright colors determines the strength and direction of the perceived motion. However, this motion disappears as soon as you try to focus on it. By staring at a fixed point within the image, the swirling motion in the peripheral vision can also be stopped.

Researchers explain this halting effect with the "perceptual stabilization" of our visual perception. Even when we concentrate on a single point, our eyes are, in reality, performing minute movements. This causes the image to shift back and forth in the retina. The brain compensates these shifts, so that they are not interpreted as movement of the object. However, in the image of the rotating snake and other motion illusions, this mechanism seems to be nullified. The brain is overtaxed by the repeating pattern and therefore generates illusionary movement.

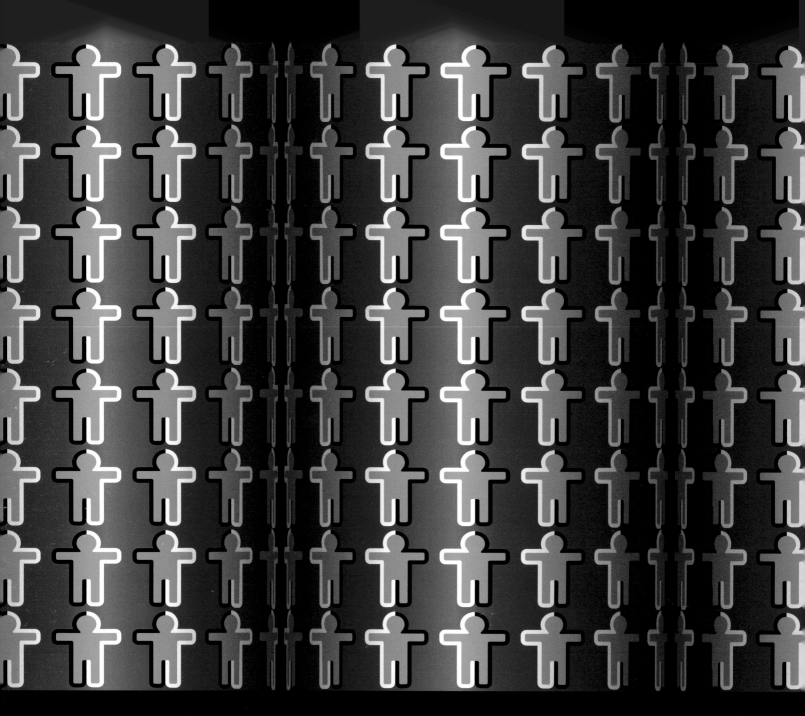

2.1 Look at one of the darker spaces between the columns.
Do you see the figures moving sideways?

While your eyes are moving across the image, it is the black and white lines
outlining the little figures that trigger this illusion. The apparent movement
comes to a halt when you squint at the image to such a degree that the color
details are unrecognizable, or when you focus on a fixed point within the
picture. According to the latest empirical findings, motion illusions such as
this one are not so much triggered by slow conscious eye movement, but

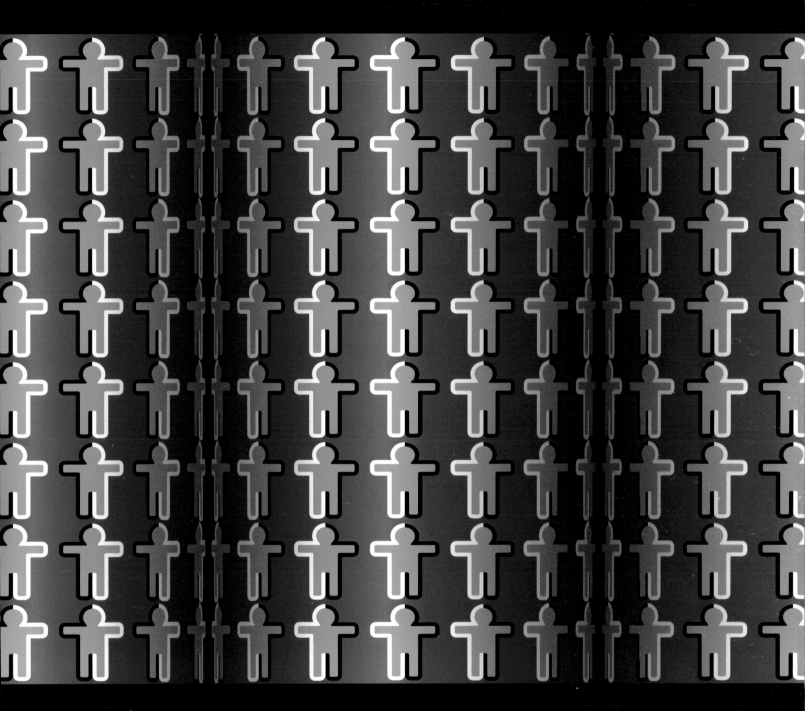

rather by the unconscious shifting around of the eyes (saccade). In order to prevent the perceived image from wobbling during this saccade, the brain suppresses our perception for a split second. At the same time, however, the repeating pattern of the illusion causes the brain to slightly lose its orientation, which it interprets as movement.

 Watch the flowers growing and the wheels spinning.

When you let your eyes wander across the pictures, the black and white outlines create a motion effect. Some effects are stronger when printed on paper, while others come to life mainly on computer or TV screens.

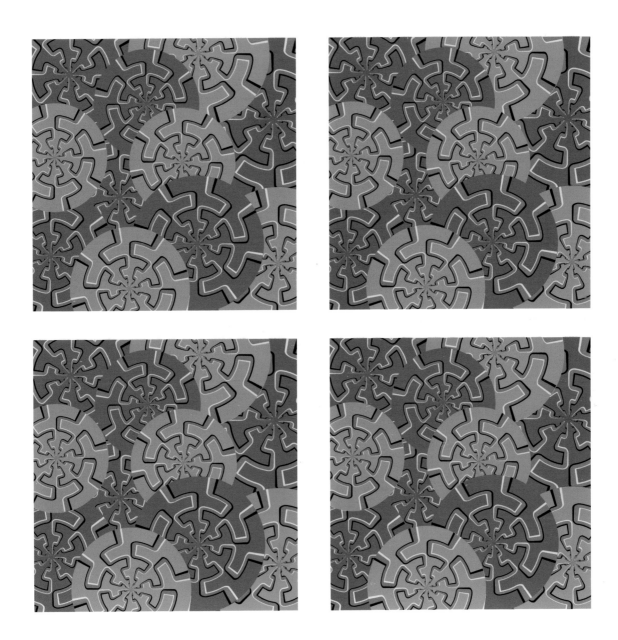

 Here are two further examples that show the subtle effects of color contrasts. Slowly move your eyes across the pictures.

The fish on the opposite page should start swimming about in their aquarium. The shimmering effect of the patterns on this page should simulate two levels: one in the foreground, the other in the back.

 2.4 **Compare the two representations of the same work of art.**

On the opposite page, the two outer strips of the image seem to move upward, while the middle strip seems to move downward (due to the different direction of the color shading). The smaller and tilted image above, however, seems much less active. It becomes apparent that size and angle do matter with optical effects.

Focus on the black dot and move your head back and forth.

Zooming In Starts the Show

This illusion of relative motion, first presented a few years ago by vision researchers Baingio Pinna and Gavin Brelstaff, is triggered by the light and dark edges of the small rhomboidal shapes. If they are interchanged, the direction in which the circles are apparently turning also changes. As in most illusions of movement, this one only works in the peripheral visual field. If you look directly at the circles, no movement can be perceived. The neuroscientific explanations are complex and disputed, though one element seems clear: illusions of motion are created in the primary visual cortex, a part of the brain located in the back of the head that specializes in pattern and motion recognition and is the first to process the information relayed from the eyes.

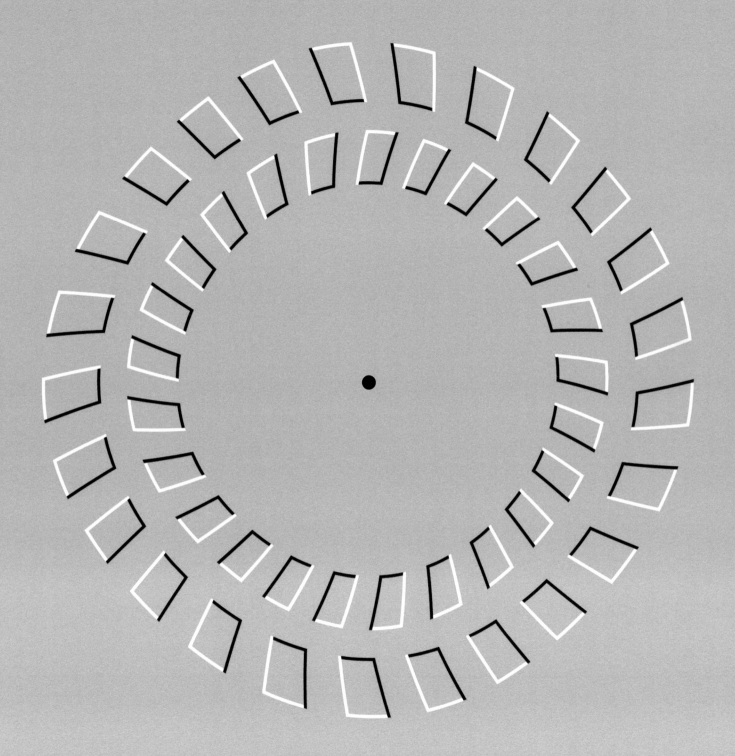

 Look at the black dot and move the book back and forth. What happens to the luminous shimmer?

This illusion, in which the size and intensity of the luminous haze seems to increase the closer you come to it, was first discovered in 2006 by psychologists Alan Stubbs and Simone Gori. Scientists have so far remained unable to determine how it is created. What has become apparent is that luminance gradient plays a crucial role. If you replace the haze with a series of concentric circles with the same graduating level of luminance, the effect is lost. The illusion can only reoccur if the number of graduating levels is increased to the extent that the impression of a smooth transition is generated.

Move the book up and down in jerks.

You can almost feel the wind driving these windmills. And yet, they are only moving in our heads. If looking at this illusion — a relative of the Rotating Snakes (page 14) — makes you feel dizzy, simply focus on any point in the picture and the little windmills will stop turning. This demonstrates the importance of minimal unconscious eye movement, or saccade, for creating such illusions of motion. Normally, saccades aid the brain in the swift comprehension of an image. Scientists are still working on the question of how saccades create imagined movement in interaction with color gradations.

At first glance, this chessboard appears to have a huge bulge protruding out of its center. Can you still play on it?

Chessboard with a Bulge

Aside from the fact that this chessboard has too many squares, playing chess on it should not be a problem, as the bulge is only an illusion generated by the white spots. No matter how much you search for an exact explanation of this illusionary phenomenon in any scientific textbook, you will not be able to find one. Like the Café Wall illusion (page 63), this phenomenon could be based on the fact that the lines of the pattern appear to bend outward due to the varying contrasts. Since we assume the chessboard to consist of a uniform pattern, our cognitive perception interprets this distortion as a bulge, protruding out toward us. What is particularly interesting here is that the spatial depth conveyed by a few scattered dots is extended over the whole area of the circle.

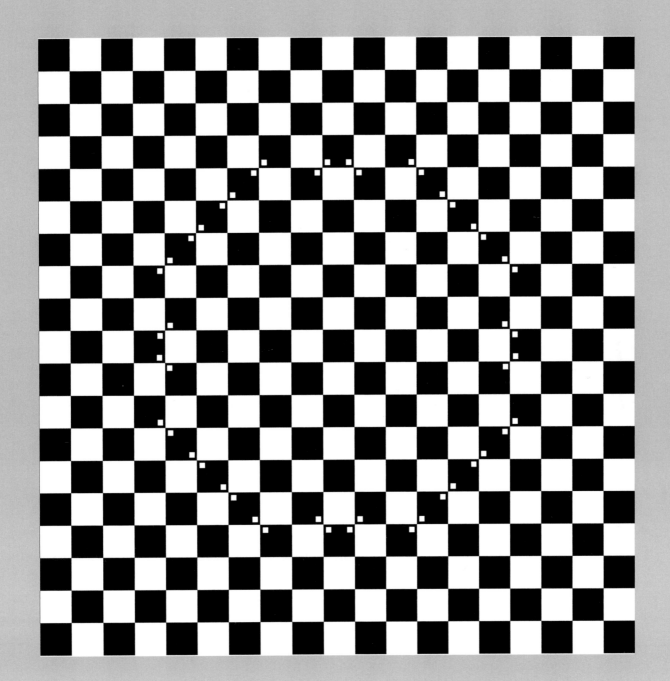

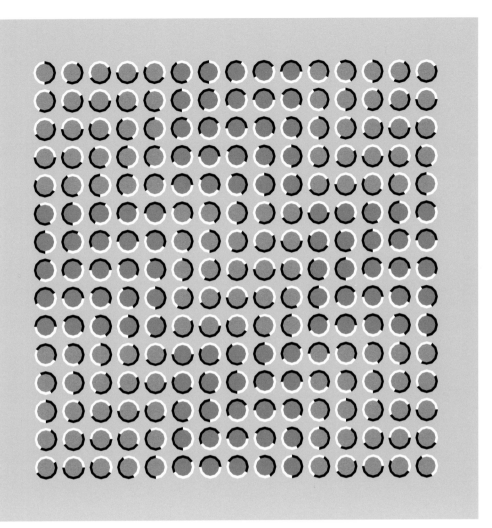

 Do you see wave movements in these pictures?

The little crosses in the image on the opposite page have a similar effect to the dots on the chessboard on page 29. Because of the regularly alternating coloring, the crosses in this picture generate a kind of wave effect. This effect, however, is not tied to the graphic element itself (cross). In the image above, two contrasting semicircles set on differently tinted circles generate the same illusion of wave movement.

 **Let your eyes wander over this pattern. Do you see a flickering?**

Seeing Things that Are Not There

As a guest in the BBC studio in the late 1950s, British physicist and neuroscientist Donald Mackay first discovered this effect on a partition wall. Employees of the studio had already noticed those ghostly shadows that seemed to flit up and down in the white areas between the line-columns. The effect seems to increase when the pattern is looked at using both eyes. Apparently, the number of identical lines makes the brain lose its focus. Thus, the brain is unable to merge the input of both eyes into the unified visual impression, with which we normally perceive the world around us.

5.1 Let your eyes wander to the center of the image. Can you see how light effects vibrate around inside the violet rings?

As in most illusions of movement, tiny, unconscious rapid eye movements (saccades) also play a key role in this so-called Enigma illusion. It becomes apparent that saccades are at play, as the effect decreases when focusing on a particular point within the center, which is due to the reduction of saccades. However, they cannot be suppressed completely. Despite numerous scientific theories, it has yet to be explained how the nexus of photoreceptor cells in the eyes and the further processing in the visual cortex create a false perception of movement.

Nevertheless, researchers at the Barrow Neurological Institute in Phoenix, Arizona, were able in 2008 to determine that saccades play an important role in this optical illusion. The notion that movement is necessarily a product of processes inside the brain has since been disproved.

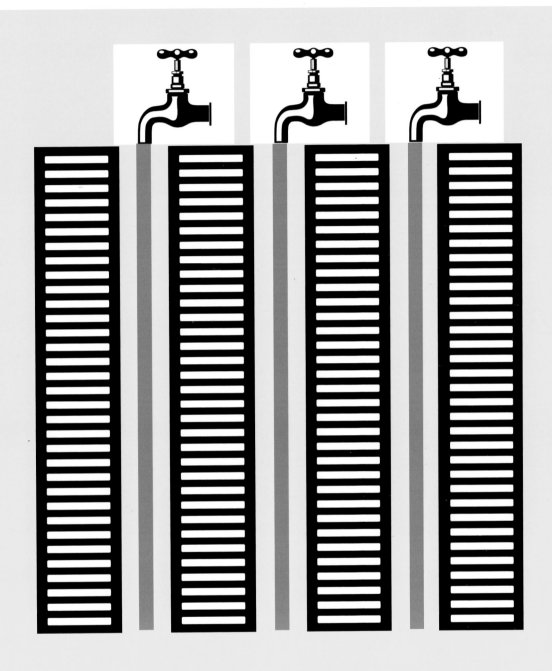

 Let your eyes wander over these images. What do you see?

In the illustration on the left page, short gray lines should be flashing in the white areas.
In the picture above, you should see the blue lines vibrating like streams of bathwater.

Let your eyes wander over the page. What is happening to the circle?

The blurred circle stands out from the sharply defined, speckled surrounding area as being restless and seemingly in motion. It is left to the observer to decide whether the circle is above or below the surface.

Two effects seem to be at play here. The unconscious shifting around of the eyes (saccades, see page 17) creates the impression of movement, while the brain interprets the fuzziness as an out-of-focus area that must be either in the background or the foreground.

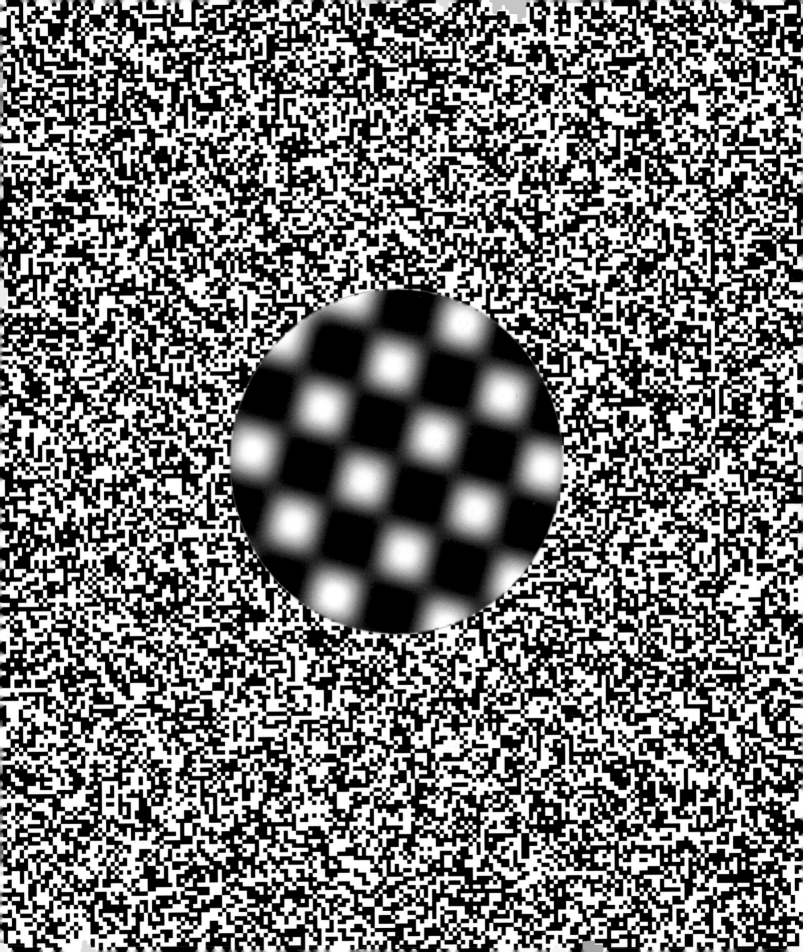

A friendly Albert Einstein is looking at us. But if we look at him from a distance, or squint our eyes, we suddenly see someone else. Do you recognize who she is?

The False Bottom of Eye Vision

When viewed up close, we see a portrait of Albert Einstein. But when we look at the image from further away, or squint our eyes, the portrait of the renowned physicist turns into Marilyn Monroe. Developed by scientists at MIT and the University of Glasgow, hybrid images consisting of two pictures of differing sharpness were superimposed on top of each other. Seen up close, the fine lines dominate. It is not until they are no longer visible from a distance that the mind gives prominence to the blurred contours.

Harvard neurobiologist Margaret Livingstone also sees this as the explanation for Mona Lisa's enigmatic smile. The smile is primarily indicated in the blurred shadows at the corners of the mouth, which are better perceived by peripheral vision. When her mouth is looked at directly, however, the smile disappears like a faint star in the sky.

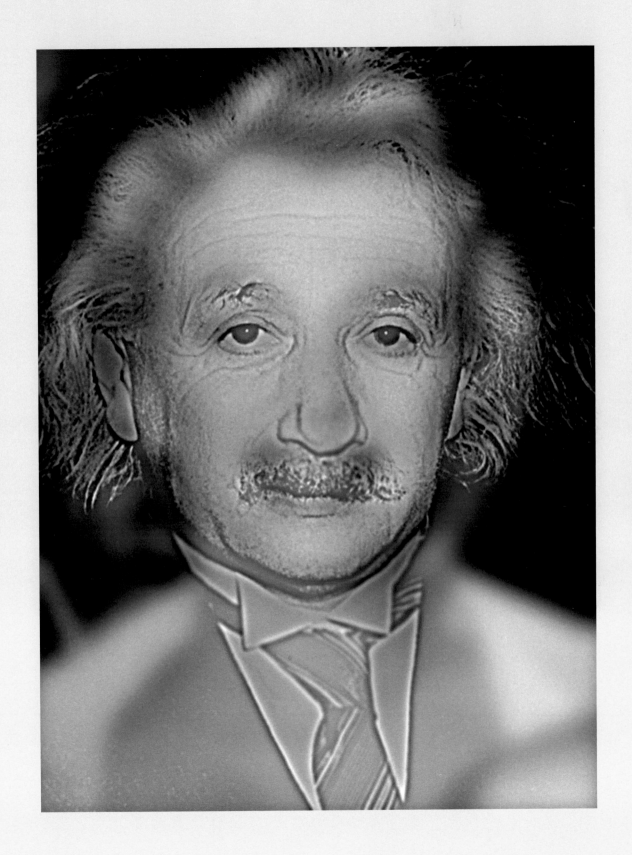

 **Which of the two photos shows the campanile tilting more to the right?**

The More Lopsided Tower of Pisa

To most observers, the tower on the right side appears to have a greater angle of tilt.
In reality, both photos are absolutely identical. This illusion demonstrates how the brain turns a two-dimensional projection on our retina into a three-dimensional image of our environment.

Our spatial perception is largely based on experience and is therefore not only a physical process, but also a mental achievement. Thus, we know that objects further away project a smaller image on the retina, and close-up objects block the view of objects further away. We also know the effect of converging lines: parallel lines, such as railroad tracks, appear to converge at a vanishing point on the horizon. This is the very effect that plays a trick on us with the Pisa towers. Since the axes in both photos do not converge, we wrongly perceive them as divergent, causing the building in the photo on the right to appear more lopsided.

Interestingly, this trick only works with objects in space, and more specifically with objects we know to have converging lines (such as the objects on the opposite page and the next double pages). It does not work with small objects or people we know to be two dimensional, as demonstrated in the image below.

Like on the previous page, two identical photos appear to be taken from two different angles.

Compare the two chess squares A and B. One is a dark shade of gray, while the other is a light gray. Or so it seems.

Locals Aren't Always Right

Whether you believe it or not, both squares are the same shade of gray. Check for yourself by covering up the area around the two squares with a sheet of paper or your hands. Because we see the image as a three-dimensional scene lit from the top right, square B in the shadow of the green cylinder appears substantially lighter. In the given example by Edward Adelson, a researcher at MIT, the effect is increased by the uniform checkered pattern of the chessboard. However, the illusionary effect also works with less predictable patterns. Local color does not have an absolute value, but depends on its context.

　　This effect helps us to perceive the world around us — independently of local lighting conditions. A darkly printed figure does reflect significantly more light in the sunlight than a piece of white paper would in the moonlight. Fortunately, however, we can still always see black figures on a white background, as our perception does not deal with absolute luminance values, but rather with relative brightness.

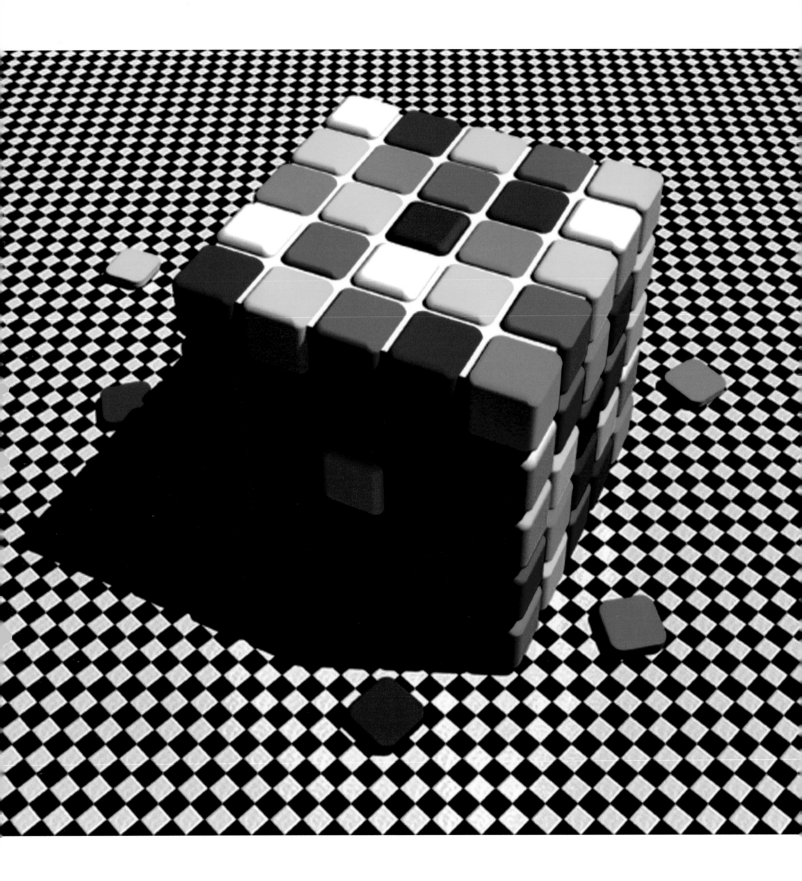

48

 The shades of gray at the top of the eggs are all different, and the square in the middle of the front side of the cube is bright orange, while the middle one on the top is dark brown. Or do you see it differently?

If you look at the eggs and the two squares through a little hole in a piece of paper, you will notice that the gray shades are identical and that both squares have exactly the same color. The cube illusion, designed by Beau Lotto and Dale Purves from Duke University, shows how the brain can perceive the same color differently, according to its context. Since the front side appears to be in shadow, the brain corrects the color accordingly. With the aid of this perception correction process, an integrated visual image of the object is created in our brain that is independent of random things like momentary lighting conditions.

 Are this manga girl's eyes really two different colors, one blue and one gray?

Undoubtedly you are thinking that if this were the case, she would hardly be included in this collection — and you are right! Seen objectively, both eyes are the exact same shade of gray. However, the left eye appears to be the same turquoise color as the hairclip, because of the red color filter placed over the left half of the image. Since the red-toned surrounding is lacking blue components, the image processing centers in the brain assume the gray of the left eye to be an intense blue. Under normal circumstances, this would be the case. Once the filter is blocked out around the eye (see above), the color of the left eye looks as gray as it actually is.

Do you see white disks behind dark clouds in the left illustration, and dark disks behind a shroud of fog on the right?

Take a closer look. The discs in both pictures are absolutely identical! The difference between the two images is the varying lightness of the surroundings. The two discoverers of this effect, the visual scientists Barton Anderson and Jonathan Winawer, attribute this to the fact that the brain tries to interpret what it sees as segmented multiple layers. However, the image must also show a coherent unity. If you turn the background image by 90 degrees, the coherent image of clouds is broken and, with it, the illusionary effect (see below).

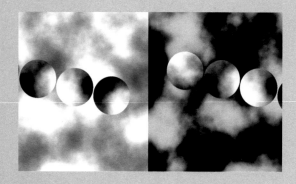

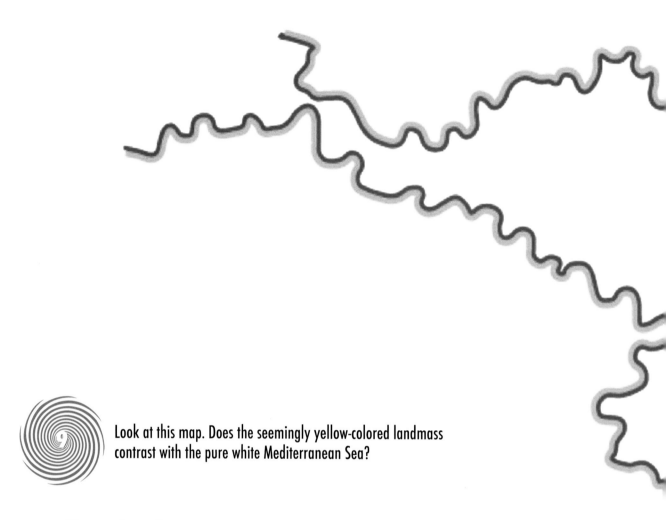

Look at this map. Does the seemingly yellow-colored landmass contrast with the pure white Mediterranean Sea?

Creating Space

This illusion by Baingio Pinna from the University of Sassari in Sardinia is based on contours that are delineated by a dark violet line and a directly adjacent yellow line running parallel to it on a white background. The areas in this image facing the yellow line seem to fill up with a yellow haze, while the violet-delineated areas remain white.

The coloration effect, which is amplified by the meandering lines, can fill amazingly large areas. Though Pinna's illusion can be produced very easily, the neurophysiological explanation proves defiantly complex. It is easier to explain what this neuronal watercolor mechanism is generally good for: shaded areas are given slightly more spatial emphasis by the brain. Our perception determines at an early stage what is to be classified as a potentially interesting object and what is to be classified as uninteresting background.

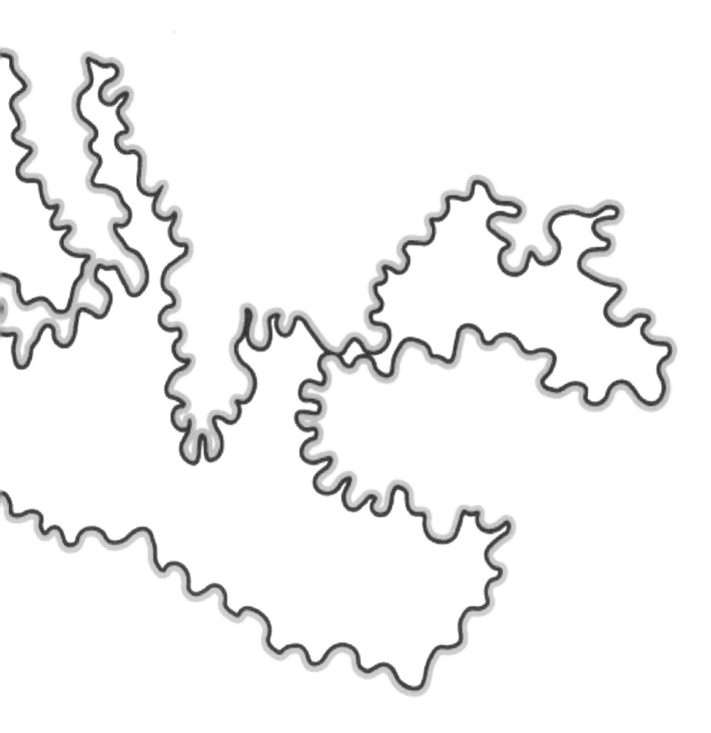

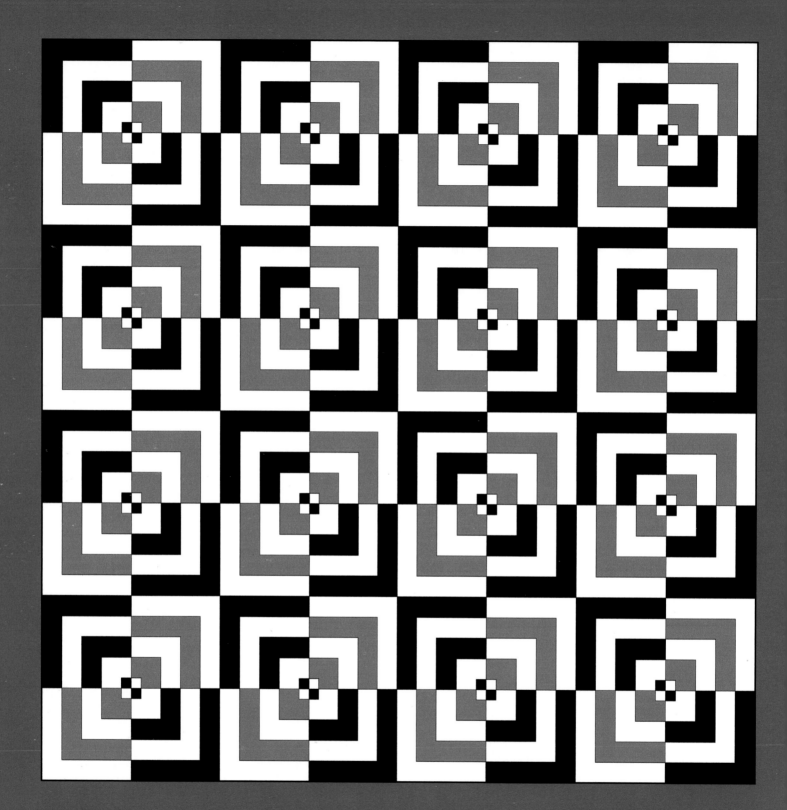

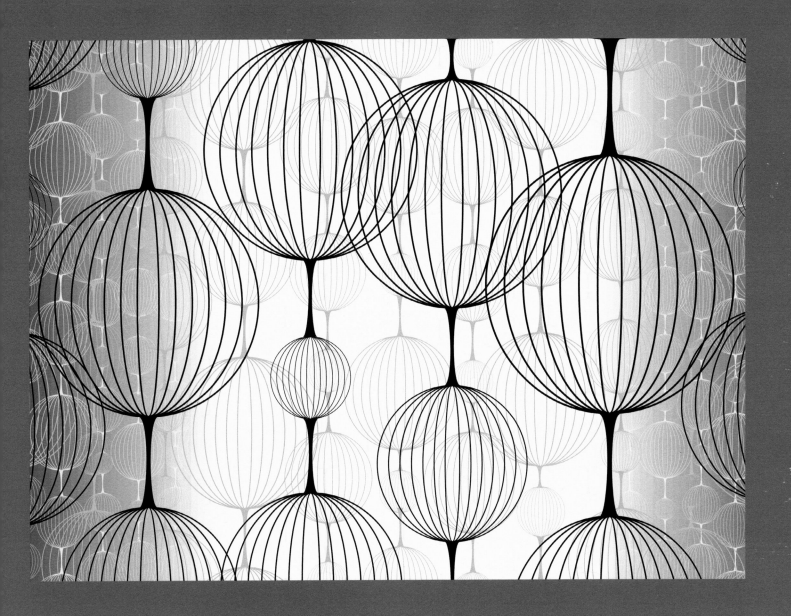

9.1 What's happening in the foreground and in the background?

Dark areas are perceived as being elevated — or being in the fore-ground — and objects of equal size seem larger the closer they are to the viewer. In the process, the mind creates a three-dimensional image. But the two illustrations shown here confuse our visual experience: each picture element could be both in the front and the back. Here, the mind must decide whether the picture is three-dimensional and how to interpret it without reliable information.

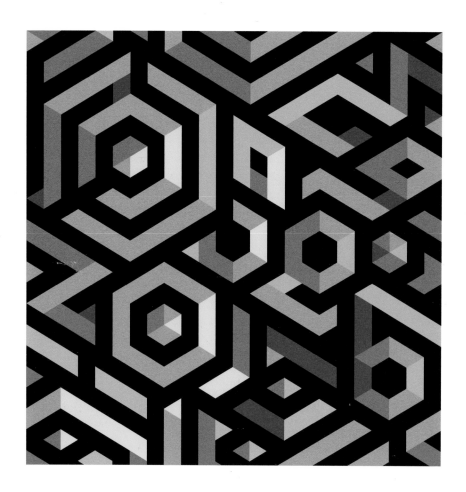

 What do you see in these two graphics — two-dimensional or three-dimensional patterns?

Our minds never tire of spatially interpreting what we see and often understand lines and colored areas to be of three-dimensional spatial depth. The patterns depicted above and opposite also trigger this impulse, but on closer examination, they prove to be completely flat and two-dimensional.

 If you can see only concentric lines and shaded areas here, hold the book further away and squint your eyes a little.

Despite the radical reduction of the images to thick and thin lines or gray tiles, you will quickly recognize our planet (above) and the most famous face in Renaissance art (opposite page). Your mind has compared the sparse information provided with images stored in memory. Media technology has made use of this cognitive feat in things like television screens and radar equipment.

Do the gray mortar lines between the black and the white tiles really begin to converge?

Crooked Parallels

This illusion is called the Café Wall illusion. Researchers at the University of Bristol discovered it in the early 1970s in the tiled wall of a café close to where they worked. The gray lines of "mortar" play a decisive role in creating this illusion. They are clearly visible where two white or black tiles meet. The eye is apparently overtaxed by the closely-spaced gradations of luminance at the place where two tiles of different colors meet and perceives the mortar line as part of the tile laying either above or below it. They appear higher on one side and therefore slightly trapezoid in form. Since these pseudo-trapezoids cannot logically be delineated by parallel lines, we interpret them as alternatingly inclining to the right or to the left.

However, for nearly 40 years, researchers have been racking their brains over the exact neuronal basis of the Café Wall illusion.

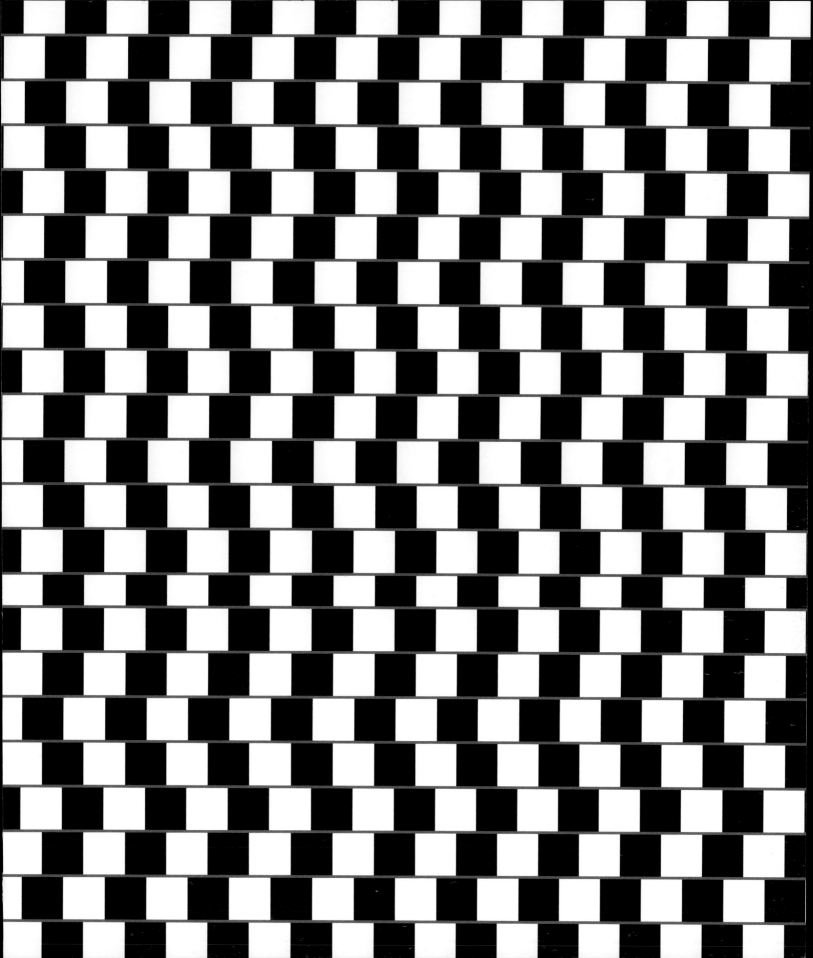

10.1 Colors make the Café Wall illusion (page 63) even more fascinating.

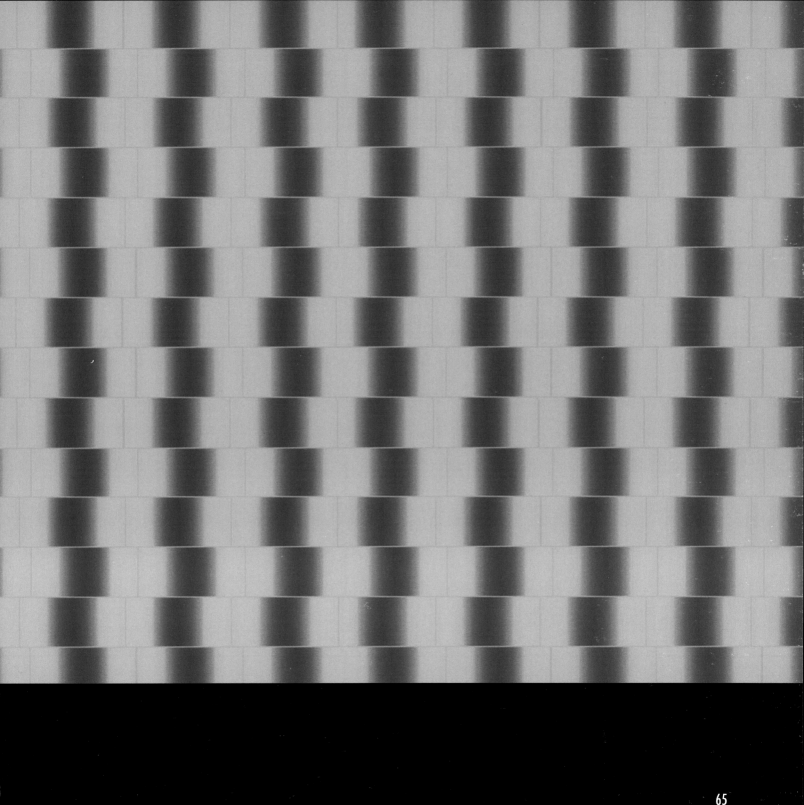

Do the long lines run parallel to each other or do they converge?

The Barbed Wire illusion can be traced back to German physicist Johann Karl Friedrich Zöllner, who published it in 1860 in a scientific journal. Why the lines, which are actually parallel to each other, appear to converge, has not yet been explained satisfactorily. Interestingly, the illusion weakens when the background is colored green and the lines are colored red in the same degree of lightness. Apparently, the contrast between foreground and background plays as decisive role.

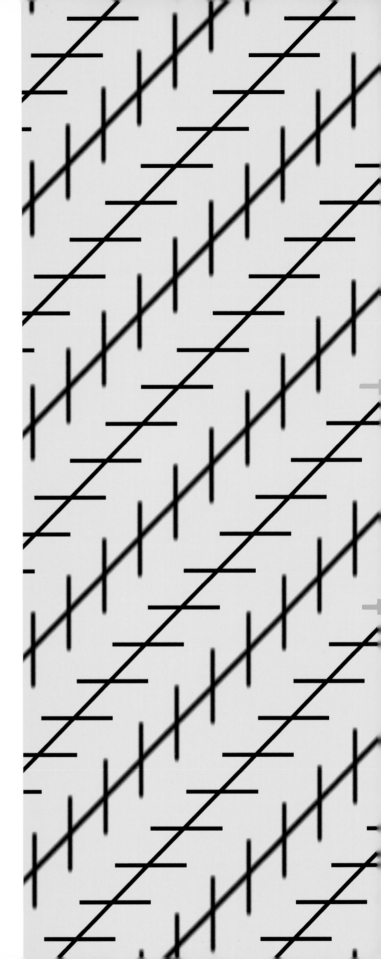

 **Normally, and outside this book, we would probably all be sure that these stripes are not parallel.**

But they are, and why they appear as if they were converging is still a scientific mystery in the tradition of the Barbed Wire illusion (page 66).

11 A clear case! Here, a black and white spiral is winding its way into the depths of space in accordance with all the rules of geometry — or is it?

Archimedes's Nightmare

The Fraser spiral, which actually consists of concentric circles, was first described in 1908 by English psychologist Sir James Fraser. Sometimes it is also called the twisted cord illusion, because the circles are reminiscent of a cord made up of black and white strands. This twisted pattern helps to create the illusion. Because the individual black and white elements tilt toward the middle in a more acute angle than the circle in which they are located, we perceive them as a spiral of decreasing diameter. This only works because the larger number of circles and the same-shaped pattern in the background make it difficult to concentrate on the individual circles.

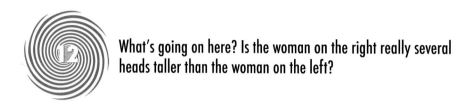

What's going on here? Is the woman on the right really several heads taller than the woman on the left?

Unequal Friends

Both women are of a completely average size. What is deviating from the norm here is the completely crooked room. Its right wall is substantially shorter and lower than the left one, and the floor is sloping upward toward the right wall. However, the tiles on the floor and the pictures on the back wall are painted in a distorted way that makes the Ames Room (named after the American ophthalmologist Adelbert Ames) appear to be a normal room when viewed from a certain angle. Since we perceive the room as normal, we can only come to one conclusion: something must be wrong with the people.

Since the woman on the right is much closer to the observer than the woman on the left, she projects a larger image on the retina. And because the surrounding room suggests that both people are standing at an equal distance from us, this fools our brains into thinking that the woman on the right is taller. The Ames Room demonstrates a fundamental problem in our visual perception. It needs to reconstruct a three-dimensional world from the two-dimensional image on our retina. And a lot can go wrong in the process.

12.1 Do you know why your brain gets confused by sizes?

Our perception of size depends both on the actual dimensions of an object and on the distance between the object and the viewer. In two dimensions, however, size depends on context, which can be subject to the interpretation of the beholder. The Sphinx appears to be the same size as the woman, who is actually much smaller, because this photo does not reveal the space in between them. On the other hand, the two figures on the opposite page, although identical in size, seem different, because the grid of converging lines creates the illusion of a deep space in which the second person is far away.

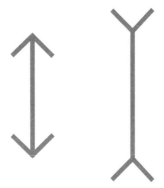

 Compare the green and blue lines on the opposite page. Which of the two is the longer line?

Most people see the blue line as being longer, although the two lines are of equal length. The laws of perspective tell us that the line at the top, located at the far back, must stretch across a considerably longer space than the line at the bottom. Accordingly, this knowledge clearly influences our estimation of the lengths of the lines.

This illusion is similar to the classic example of optical illusions: the Müller-Lyer illusion (see above), in which the right line appears to be longer. Apparently, we compare the total length of the arrow on the right — including its ends — with the length of the left shaft.

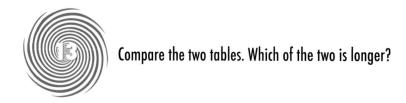 **Compare the two tables. Which of the two is longer?**

When Perspective Is Swept under the Table

Don't let the tables fool you. These two tabletops designed by Roger Shepard from Stanford University are actually absolutely identical. If you don't believe it, measure them for yourself. The rules of perspective are to blame for the tabletop on the left appearing longer and narrower. The rules say that a more distant object appears smaller and that parallel lines, like those of a tabletop, converge more closely the further away they get.

Our vision system, which must constantly construct a three-dimensional world out of two-dimensional images on the retina, compensates entirely automatically for the distorted image. The correction mechanism makes these tables, drawn with incorrect perspective, appear to be skewed and of a different size.

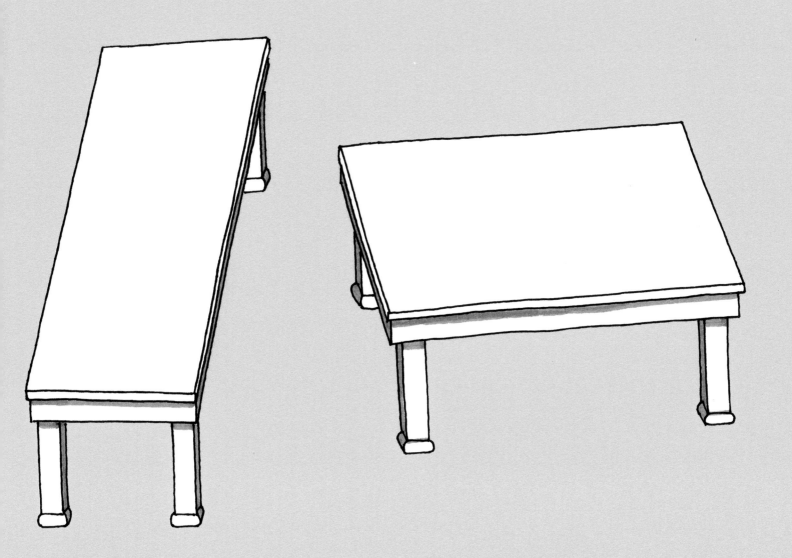

Nothing in this photo was touched up. However, a Beuchet chair was used. Can you figure out what its secret is?

Although the Beuchet chair appears to be a regular chair, it actually consists of two separate elements that are placed at different distances from the viewer. The man is squatting on the over-sized seat of the chair and both he and the seat are placed at the back of the room. Seen from the right angle, this part fits perfectly on the normal-sized legs of the chair, which are located some distance closer to the viewer. Since we see the chair as one complete object, the man sitting on it appears to be tiny.

 **Compare the two orange circles. Which one is larger?**

Among Giants and Dwarfs

The orange circle on the left appears to be smaller than the one on the right. They are, however, the same size.

Context-dependent illusions, such as the identical circles first described by the German psychologist Hermann Ebbinghaus (1850–1909), are strongly based on our visual experience and memory. Therefore, the effect depends on the observer. It takes children, for instance, a number of years to gain the visual experience required to become receptive to the illusion induced by contrasting sizes.

Cultural differences also appear to have an effect on the illusion's strength, as a comparative study of the Ebbinghaus illusion has demonstrated. Thus, people from Japan seem to experience the supposed difference in size more strongly than people from Central Europe. This brings up the cliché of the holistic-minded Asians, who pay much more attention to context than Europeans do. On the other hand, members of the Himba tribe in Namibia are barely susceptible to the illusion at all. Whether this has anything to do with the Himba's more individualistic view of the world has remained undetermined.

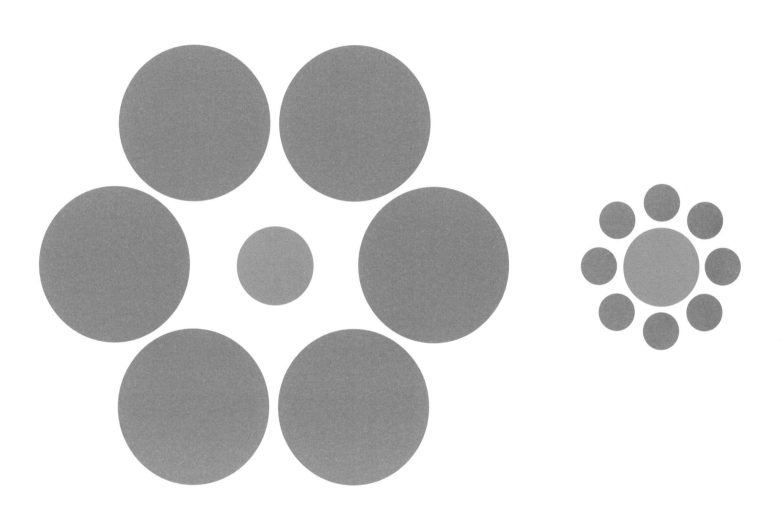

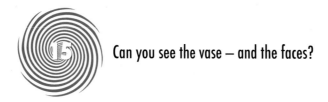

Can you see the vase — and the faces?

Look Who's Hiding

Rubin's vase is a classic optical illusion, seen here in a modern version. It dates back to Danish psychologist Edgar Rubin (1886–1951), who undertook close studies of the phenomenon of multistable perception using ambiguous figures. In this picture, we can either see a vase in front of a dark background, or two silhouettes of faces looking at each other. Our perception involuntarily jumps from one interpretation of the image to the other. Once again, behind it all is our pronounced tendency to interpret what we see, to separate the essential from the nonessential, and to suppress inconsistencies as much as possible.

15.1 This color etching from the 19th century shows not only a couple of pretty violets, but also Napoleon Bonaparte, his second wife Marie Louise of Austria, as well as their son. Can you find them all?

According to legend, when he was exiled to the island of Elba in 1814, Napoleon promised he would return "when the violets bloom in the spring." Consequently, his followers demonstrated their support with bouquets of violets and violet-colored clothing when "Corporal Violet" returned to Paris, as announced, in March of 1815.

Ambiguous figures such as this one, designed by French painter Jean-Dominique-Etienne Canu, were all the rage at the time. Because they force us to choose what we see in the image — the faces or the flowers (it seems impossible to see both at the same time) — they remain a favored method in psychological research in the study of key mental abilities (such as attention) up to the present day.

 Can you see a young and an old woman above?

The illustration *My Wife and My Mother-In-Law* (above) by the cartoonist William Ely Hill is the classic of ambiguous figures; it was published in 1915 in the American satirical magazine *Puck*. On the opposite page, you see both a (half) frontal view and a side view of a young woman. Doesn't she look like straight out of one of Picasso's cubist paintings?

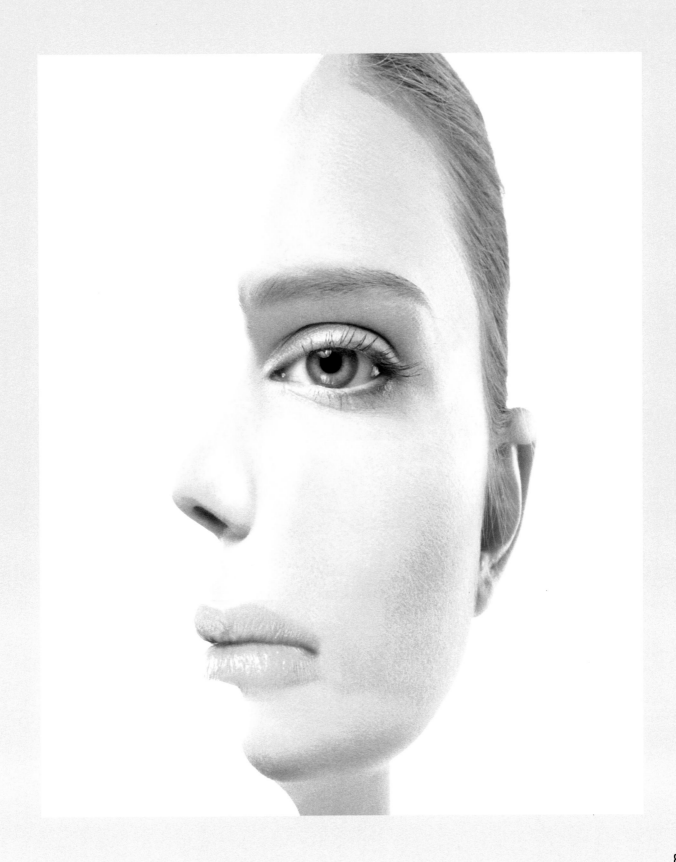

These pictures show two schemes each. Can you see them?

You will easily discover the young lady in front of a mirror on the opposite page. But looking again, you may see the whole picture as one big skull. Can you also see the saxophone player and/or the girl in the left-hand illustration above? What about the rabbit and/or the duck on the right?

 **Do you see clouds or a face?**

Faces Everywhere

Pareidolia is what psychologists call people's propensity to give meaning to everything they see. This tendency is especially pronounced with anything that remotely resembles a human face. Even if it is just a simple arrangement of characters like a colon, dash and parenthesis — presto, you have **:-)** a happy face that can be used as an emoticon for emails or text messages.

This is of no surprise to researchers, since the recognition of faces is of particular importance to social beings like humans. Special areas of the brain constantly search through all the available visual information for faces. If these brain areas are injured, the sufferer loses the ability to differentiate between faces and to interpret facial expressions. Neurologists call this *prosopagnosia*, or face blindness.

We not only interpret faces into things, but also feelings.

Whether we see a tired dog in rocks on a shoreline, or a surprised face in an electrical outlet depends on our individual fantasies. However, the fact that there are widespread patterns of recognition, which work even when reduced to a minimum, can be seen in a strange quirk from history: many people around the globe see Adolf Hitler in even the vaguest combination of a straight thick line and another at an angle — such as the (unintended) example of a tea kettle by Michael Graves.

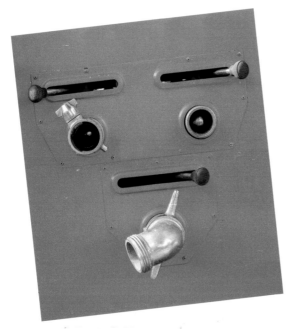

 ## Are you able to NOT see the faces?

Spanish surrealist Salvador Dalí repeatedly turned the American actress Mae West into the subject of his work — most recently in 1972 in this walk-in room in his Theater-Museum in Figueres, Spain. The lip sofa that was specifically created for this room is still available in specialized design shops and has been copied many times. The fireplace in the form of a nose, however, never made it into mass production.

Actually, it is the lips in these two pictures that make it so difficult for a viewer to separate the individual elements of the pictures from their context and see several flowers with a butterfly, or the interior of a room. The key stimulus of the lips overpowers the ability to perceive what is actually being shown.

If these faces look pretty much the same to you then turn the book around ...

Upside Down

Face recognition is one of the specialties of human perception. However, we are calibrated to see faces in a normal upright position. If they are upside down, as in this photo, slight deviations, such as inverted eyes and mouths, escape us. This is an effect that Peter Thompson from the University of York, England, discovered in 1980. According to one current theory, in facial recognition we analyze the details of individual elements (like the shape of the nose) and their relative position to one another (like how close together the eyes are or where the ears are). This configuration perception is impaired, making deviations hardly noticeable when the face is turned upside down. This changes when in a normal upright position: the upside down mouth and eyes make the face appear completely deformed due to our fine sense for faces.

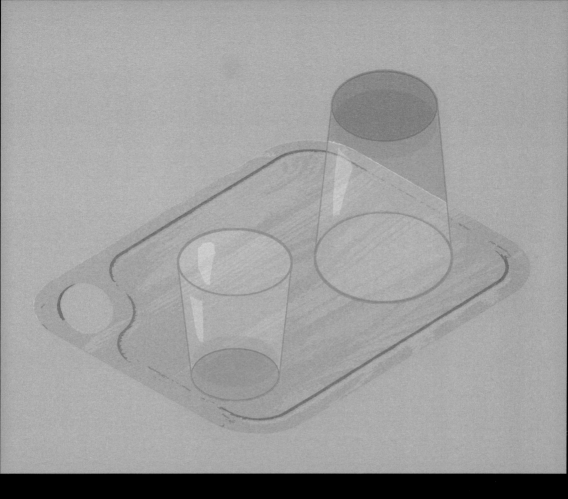

 17.1 Do you see a futuristic subway platform on the opposite page? Are both glasses on the tray? Turn the book around to get another view of things.

The photo on the left shows stairs leading down to the Zollverein coal mine, in the German city of Essen. It was named a UNESCO World Cultural Heritage Site in 2001. The picture above clearly demonstrates the difficulties our brains have in interpreting a two-dimensional view as a three-dimensional space.

 The next time you visit a museum, you may be surprised at what you find. Can you see the hidden skulls in these paintings?

The Art of Tricking the Eye

For centuries artists have used various elements to create optical illusions in their art, and they continue to do so to this day. In Salvador Dalí's painting on the opposite page, a group of women turn into the bust of the philosopher Voltaire. In the image above, 16th-century painter Hans Holbein placed a distorted and tilted image of a skull in the foreground of his painting *The Ambassadors*. Seen from the right angle, the skull eventually shrinks into its correct shape.

So you think there are no optical illusions in this photograph?

Though they are fairly subtle ones, they do exist! And they are almost 2,500 years old.

Constructing a building this close to perfection meant that the Greek master builders had to cheat a little around the corners and in the center of the building. The four columns located at the corners are in closer proximity to their neighboring columns (by about 10 percent) than the other columns are to one another. Furthermore, the columns are leaning toward the center of the building and instead of tapering linearly have a "swelling" shaft, which makes them appear more solid and stable than they actually are. Additionally, many of the major ancient temples bend slightly upward toward the middle, because straight architectural forms, when very long, tend to look as though they are sagging.

Without the help of computers or any scientific research, Greek master builders managed to construct perfectly harmonious, large-scale buildings, simply by employing optical illusions.

 ## Roman 3D mosaic – authentic or fake?

They may have been brushed up a little, but these mosaics are authentic Roman works of art. The dog that casts a shadow with its forelegs is guarding a villa in Pompeii, and the impressive three-dimensional mosaic on the right was part of a second century BC Roman house in Malta.

 In the ceiling fresco on the opposite page, it almost seems as though the potted plant and several cherubs could fall down onto the observer at any moment.

In classical antiquity, artists knew how to generate a stark impression of spatial depth on a two-dimensional surface (see page 103). By the Middle Ages, this art form had been forgotten. It wasn't until the Renaissance that it was rediscovered by painters interested in the sciences, such as Mantegna, who decorated the Palazzo Ducale in Mantua (opposite page), or Bramante, who created the image and illusion of a very deep choir on an almost flat wall in a church in Milan (above). Today, in times of photo wallpapers and huge TV screens, the effect of their frescos may appear charmingly peculiar. In the 15th century, however, their contemporaries would touch the wall when studying the frescos, to find out if there really was a wall or if they were looking into another room.

Mantegna used the simple form of a central perspective in which all elements (e.g., the balustrade) converge on a central vanishing point. Shortly thereafter, artists like da Vinci und Dürer developed more complicated perspective constructs, such as the bird's-eye view, the worm's-eye view and the multipoint perspectives.

18.4 Giving architects free reign ...

This house, which was apparently overturned by a hurricane, is the distinctive main building of a family adventure park in Orlando, Florida, and was designed in 1998 by architect Terry Nicholson. It quickly became so famous that the owner and operator, Wonderworks, copied the idea to other sites and now has had four such baffling museum buildings built.

Vincenzo Scamozzi went about it more subtly 500 years earlier in the Teatro Olimpico in Vicenza, with openings showing a view of city streets behind it. The architect whimsically played with the perspective by setting up three different lines of sight, and thereby creating the illusion of a long street receding hundreds of yards into the distance. In reality, however, it is not even 40 feet deep. Scamozzi created the effect by sloping the floor upward and foreshortening the perspective with a succession of increasingly smaller sections of buildings.

18.5 The trompe l'œil — how does it work?

Italian painter Andrea Pozzo created this colossal ceiling fresco in the Church of Sant'Ignazio di Loyola in Rome in 1685. It portrays the ascension of Saint Ignatius to heaven and develops its enormous effect through the apparent extension of the walls and the opening up to the sky above. Adding to this is an extreme view from below and the accompanying drastic foreshortening of bodies and architecture. Pozzo incorporated the standpoint of the viewer into the construction of his illusionary space, making it a set point. Seen from that specific spot in the church, the space above is (sur)realistically expanded — from other spots, however, the fresco appears distorted. The dotted line indicates where the actual ceiling of the church beginns.

ET QVID VOLO NISI
VT ACCENDATVR

 Fake views

Optical illusions have been extremely popular since the Renaissance not only in churches, but also in palaces.

Although many trompe-l'œil paintings can only be viewed from one defined spot, others are kept two-dimensional and obtain their charm from imaginative visual ideas (see pages 113, 140–143).

A Mayan temple for the god against earthquakes. Mural by John Pugh in Los Gatos, California.

 Don't the famous Potemkin Stairs in Odessa (opposite) seem to go endlessly on up on the hill?

The fact is that the stairway, built in the first half of the 19th century (here in a historical photo), is a good 460 feet in length, and its 200 steps take it to a height of almost 100 feet. Actually not too bad, but the stairway made famous by Sergei Eisenstein's 1925 classic movie *Battleship Potemkin* appears to stretch all the way up the sky, thanks to a trick of perspective. The lowest step is 70 feet wide, almost twice as wide as the top step at 40 feet. The converging sides are interpreted by our perception, however, as lines converging to a vanishing point on the horizon, thereby making the stairway appear much longer than it really is. In addition, the treads of the stairs cannot be seen, which only increases the impression that they rise forever upward.

Conceived by Italian architect and sculptor Gian Lorenzo Bernini in the 17th century, St. Peter's Square in Rome (above) follows a similar concept, only vice versa: the trapezoid floor plan widens in the direction of St. Peter's Basilica, which makes the very wide facade of the basilica look smaller and the dome taller. Ultimately, the effect makes the whole building seem closer to people looking at it from the back of the square.

 Put yourself in the place of the man on the stairs. Can you find the first step?

Up and Down the Stairs

Obviously these stairs have no beginning and no end. The idea for the continuous staircase that ends in itself originated with British mathematician Roger Penrose, after whom it is named. The Penrose stairs belong to those impossible figures that only work on a two-dimensional sheet of paper.

**Turn the book in a circle
and discover the different spatial views.**

To this day, M.C. Escher remains the most important artist who worked with impossible figures. Many of his works — like the two hands drawing each other, a water canal flowing into itself, and naturally the various stair pictures — are among the icons of graphic art of the 20th century.

The picture shown here, *Relativity* of 1953, breaks away from perceptive reality and constructs a surreal space using three perspectives.

123

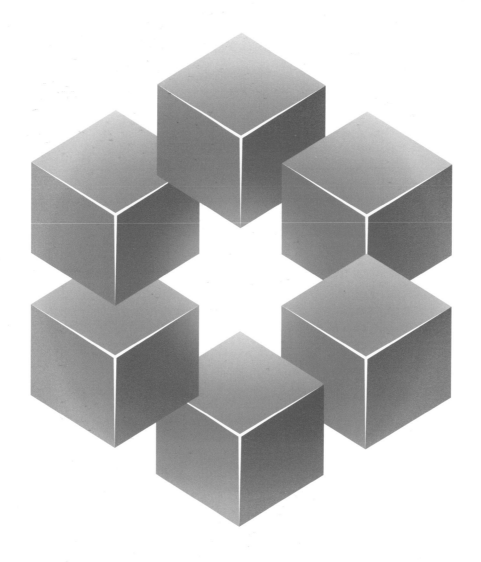

 Even rather simple impossible figures have a strong illusionary effect.

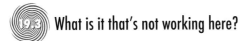 ## What is it that's not working here?

Technically, these pictures seem correct, but our minds know that neither the machine nor the domino tiles can be put together like this in a three-dimensional world.

 **A triangle of plaster? Is something not right here?**

Impossible Triangle

That's right! The depicted object could not actually exist in reality. First of all, the fact that three of the angles are right angles goes against all the basic laws of geometry. Furthermore, it seems impossible to determine which of the corners on the right side is the closest to the observer. Despite all that, such a Penrose triangle (named after British mathematician Roger Penrose) can be seen in real life. It all depends on the right perspective. See below how that is possible.

20.1 Architects in distress.

Today, architects create constructions and shapes that would not have been conceivable just a generation ago, because no contractor would have known how to build them at the time. But even today, with all the technological advances, the schemes shown below and on the opposite page are still impossible to build.

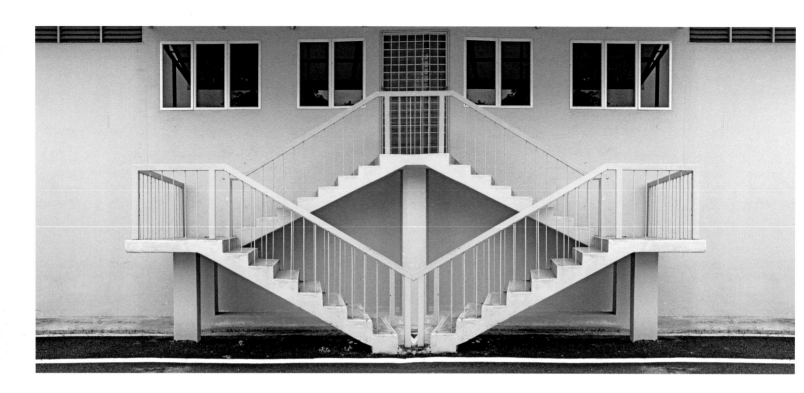

 **Look again!**

William Hogarth, an 18th-century English painter and pictorial satirist, shows a topsy-turvy world in this etching.

The photographer of the staircase above proved himself similarly cunning when he suspended reality with a minor retouching of his photo.

 **Is the woman in the picture really floating above everything?**

Uplifting Speech

In real life, the fluttering of the flag's shadow would probably have ruined the effect. But in this photo you can hardly escape coming to the conclusion that the shadow is part of the platform and, consequently, the platform must be floating a foot and a half above the sand. In addition, no other objects in the picture are casting a shadow, which would provide information about the position of the sun.

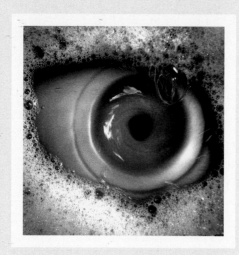

21.1 Two bodies, one head — has the African savanna produced two zebras growing from the same neck?

Actually, the head of the zebra to the left is simply hidden from view by the head of the zebra to the right. Or is it rather the other way around? This unusual perspective creates a picture puzzle that makes it difficult to determine which zebra's head we are looking at. The black and white lines so characteristic of zebras surely add to the problem. The markings serve as a form of protection for zebras. The lines confuse lions and other predators and make it more difficult for them to distinguish the outline of individual animals in a herd — a trick that works well on humans, too.

Snapshots of the real world can look rather strange in photographs. The picture above is of a sink. But that wasn't your first thought, was it?

 Can you see the creature in each of the photographs?

For many animals, camouflage is the key to survival. Blending in with their surroundings serves as a form of protection from being eaten. Others are predators themselves and wait for unsuspecting prey to get near enough to start an ambush attack. Either way, some species, like the sole above, have raised the art of camouflage to utter perfection.

 Here's looking at you, kid!

In some indigenous cultures, body painting is considered to display another (foreign) soul. Have a look at the young woman's eyes on the opposite page. Apparently, she wants to keep a close eye on her surroundings while communicating with her inner self.

 Playing tricks in real life.

Can we really trust our first impression of something? These photographs all show scenes and settings familiar to us. But after a closer examination, we notice that something has been manipulated in order to question our seeing habits. The manipulations overturn reality in a subtle and clever way.

 Right in the middle of Chongqing, a major city in Southwest China, a woman is balancing on a wire above a yawning chasm. Has this picture been manipulated?

Streetlife

Looking at this chalk street art from the side or from above (see left), it looks like nothing more than a wild design. But from the proper viewpoint, it becomes a balancing act on a wire. Covering over 9,600 sq. ft., this illusion created by the artist Qi Xinghua in 2011 was the largest piece of 3D street art in the world at the time and was entered in the Guiness Book of World Records.

The principle behind distorted pictures that only become visible from a certain angle is called anamorphosis (see pages 102–114).

 ## Strange things are taking place in the streets.

The effect of an illusion is not only based on the technical capabilities of the artist, but rather — or perhaps even more strongly — on the idea behind a picture. That is why the pictures that have the greatest effect are those that surprise us in the way we think and are used to seeing things. Street art is a temporary art; its creators often remain anonymous (left and right). Even Banksy (below), probably the most famous street artist in the world, hides behind his pseudonym and does not appear publicly, although his works have long been traded by auction houses and bought by collectors and museums.

Look at the eye of the parrot for 30 seconds and then at the center of the birdcage. What do you see?

What Comes Afterward

Suddenly, a green parrot appears to be sitting in the cage that was empty just a moment ago — a color afterimage of its red counterpart. The explanation for such complementary color afterimages is similar to the black-white variant (see page 155). While looking a the actual bird image, the retina's red photoreceptors that are being activated by the red light reduce their level of sensitivity after a few seconds. When the white light of the empty cage reaches the area accustomed to red, the photoreceptor cells specializing in red light react weakly. However, their counterparts set to blue and green react normally. The result is a blue-green color impression.

149

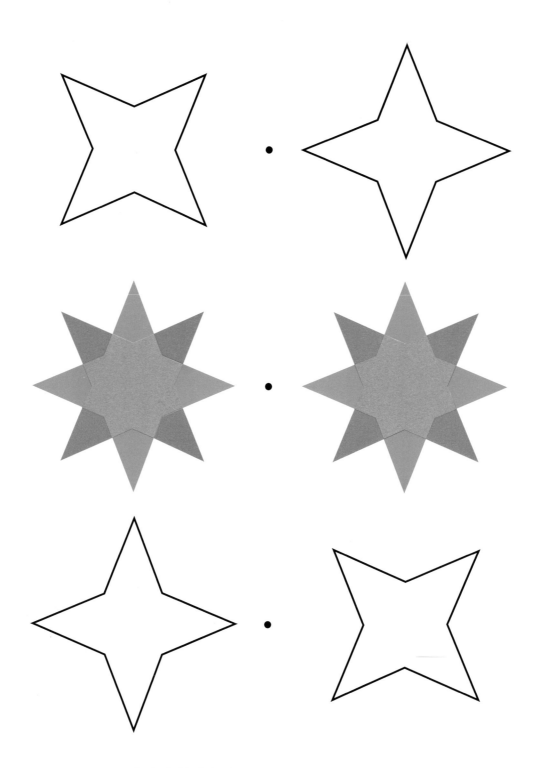

 Focus on the little black dot between the two colored stars for about 30 seconds and then focus on the dot right above it. The shape to its left should appear to have a greenish haze, while the shape to the right should have a reddish haze. The exact opposite ought to occur with the two shapes below the colored stars.

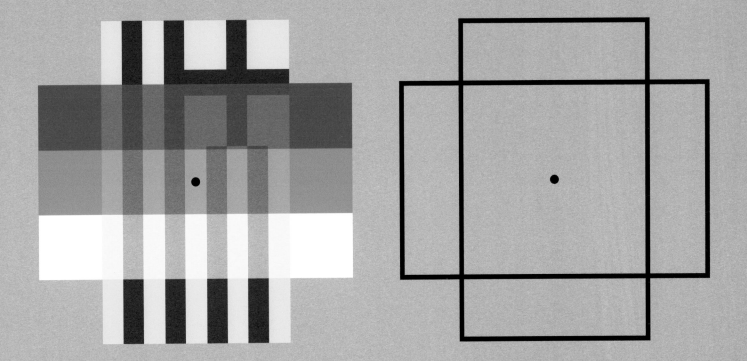

23.2 **Focus on the black dot in the left-hand image for about a minute, before immediately focusing on the dot at the center of the outlines on the right. At the same time, try to switch your attention back and forth between the horizontal and the vertical rectangles on the right. Do you notice what happens?**

You should see the German flag at first and then the Greek flag in the afterimages. This optical illusion, discovered by Peter Tse of Dartmouth College in New Hampshire, demonstrates how we can influence our perception by focusing our attention. Depending on which of the rectangles we focus on, we discern different parts of the afterimage. We can switch back and forth between the two flags until both of them fade away.

 Although afterimages are created on the eye's retina, they are then processed and interpreted by the brain. The example shown on the opposite page demonstrates this process. In this illusion, created by Rob van Lier and Mark Vergeer of Radboud University in Nijmegen, the color of the afterimage depends on the shape of the given outline. The brain seems to prefer the portions of the afterimage that fit the given outline and suppresses the part of the afterimage that does not.

Focus on the fox on the left for about 30 seconds, then focus on the fox on the right. The fox on the right now appears to be faintly reddish. Can you see it?

Afterimages, like film negatives, normally shimmer in complementary colors — bright turns into dark, red turns to blue-green. However, this is not the case in this illusion, where the effect works only if you focus on both targeted points with great precision. Without this precision, the red shimmer fades. The outline of an object seems to play a significant role in whether or not the afterimage is perceived. What is still unclear, though, is how such afterimages come about and how exactly they produce illusory colors for images whose actual colors have not changed (both foxes are white). Evidently, some complex processing level inside the brain plays a key role in this case.

Focus on one of the monkeys for about 30 seconds before you shift your gaze to a white surface. Feel free to blink a few times in between! A negative image portraying a famous evolutionary biologist should appear on the surface. Can you see it?

Afterimages such as this are produced because the photosensitive cells in the retina adapt to uniform and prolonged stimulation by reducing their sensitivity. When you look away from the original image, these areas of diminished sensitivity convey a dark afterimage. Areas at first conceived as dark now appear to be light because the photoreceptors, which have not been used yet, absorb light and relay the optical stimulation in full strength to the brain. The fine white outlines of the monkeys in the image on the right are so thinly drawn that they are no longer perceptible in the blurry afterimage.

23.5 **This illusion requires some patience, but is, in return, all the more astounding.**

Stare at the black square in the center of the striped blue disk for about
10 seconds, before focusing on the black square in the green disk for just as long.
Repeat this task at least three times so that your eyes become accustomed to both
the combinations of colors and the vertical and horizontal stripes (note that a
longer "exposure time" increases the effect).

   Now look at the black and white disks. The horizontal areas of both black and
white disks should now have a purple shimmer, while the shimmer in the vertical
areas is green. Try it again later. This effect, discovered in 1965 by American visual
perception researcher Celeste McCollough, and named after her, normally lasts
up to several hours. How it develops and why it lasts so much longer than other
afterimages has yet to be explained. The McCollough effect provides impressive
proof that our perception of form and color is linked.

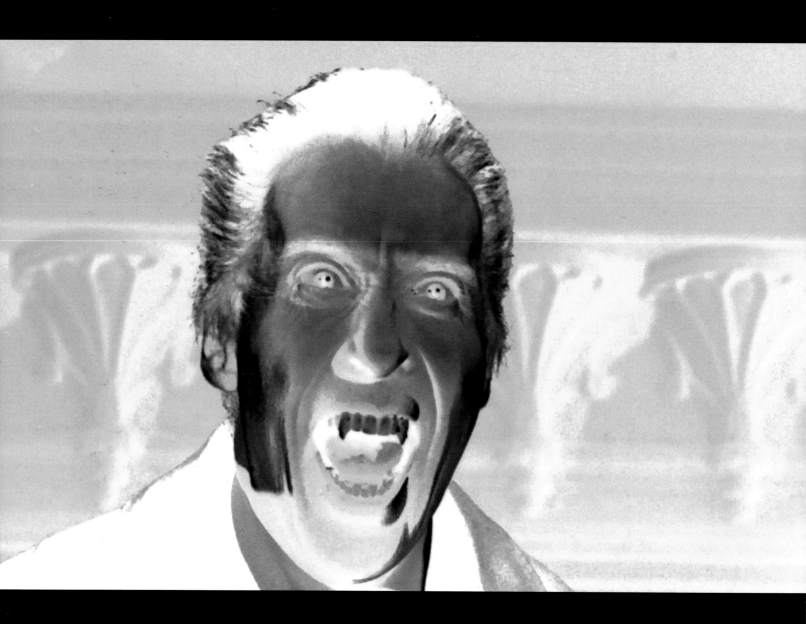

23.6 Focus on the tip of the nose of the man portrayed above for 30 seconds, then transfer your gaze further away onto a white wall. Do the same with the picture of the woman on the opposite page.

The white wall serves as a projection screen, on which the afterimage is enlarged — as is the surprise effect!

24 Is the photo of George Clooney really blue on one side and yellow on the other? Focus on the black dot on this page for about 30 seconds and then switch your gaze to the dot on Mr. Clooney's forehead. Now the stripes should have disappeared.

Star and Stripes

A split afterimage is created in this process. The cones on the left retina become accustomed to blue and the cones on the right retina to yellow, making them less sensitive to the respective colors. Thus, the afterimage shimmers in complementary colors (left: yellowish and right: bluish), more or less compensating for the missing colors in the photograph.

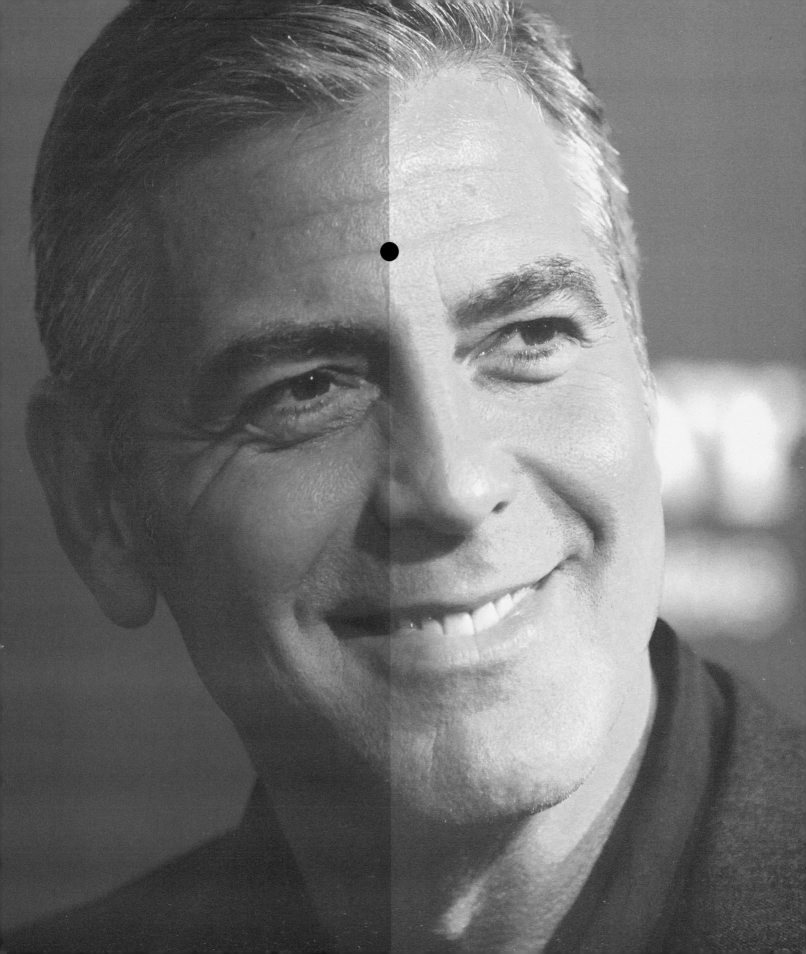

 Focus on the red dot on the car above for about a minute and then focus on the same spot in the picture on the right.

As a result, the Berlin Wall — which this Trabbi is breaking through at the famous East Side Gallery — appears in the original color of this painting: light blue.

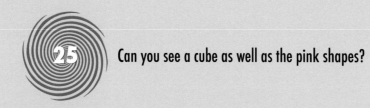

Can you see a cube as well as the pink shapes?

Shapes out of Nowhere

To be precise, there are only 24 pink shapes in this image, but our imagination, constantly seeking meaning, interprets them as pink circles in front of which the corners of a cube are delineated. Named after Italian psychologist Gaetano Kanizsa, this Kanizsa figure seems to appear out of nowhere. Such subjectively perceived contours help to form an image of a whole object retrieved from an often incomplete real world. An example of this is when an object is partially hidden from view, as it appears to be the case here. Our ability to supplement the unseen seems to be mostly innate; even babies have the ability, as do a large number of animals.

Can you see the dog? Do you recognize anything in this sea of black splotches?

It may take you a while to discover the dalmation sniffing the ground, but as soon as you do, it will seem as though you had been looking at a normal picture all along. Once again, this illusion illustrates how complex the tasks are that the brain must master in order to generate a meaningful image of the world from what is often confusing information retrieved by the eye. In the process, the brain has to differentiate between essential and unimportant information.

⟳ **Can you identify the two people in the image on the left? And can you make out what is happening in the image above?**

Hidden in the mosaic on the left are Bill and Hillary Clinton — sometimes referred to jointly as Billary. The image above depicts two movie snapshots combined to suggest a single scene in which a young woman witnesses a burglary and calls the police for help.

These picture puzzles demonstrate that the human brain is capable of rearranging pieces of visual information into a whole. Without this ability we would be unable to safely cross a road, let alone drive a car.

 **Isn't it astonishingly easy to read the text on the opposite page, despite the many jumbled words?**

Alphabetical Jumble

Only in the early stages of learning to read are people forced to decipher each individual letter of a word and then piece them together. With experience, however, we skip many letters, even entire words. As a result, we often overlook typing or spelling errors. Reading the text on the opposite page poses no difficulty because it is made up of short, common words. Many words (the, it, in, is) were not changed and the grammatical structure was retained. In order to understand longer words, however, we need more than just the first and last letters to make sense of them. It requires some effort to decipher "ahaptibecall jlmube" as the title of this text.

Wehn reandig it deos not meattr in what odrer the letrtes in a wrod are, as lnog as the fsrit and the lsat ltteer are at the crecort psiotoin. Tihs is so besacue we do not raed ecah leettr iivinddually, but the wrod as a wlohe.

can you find the the mistake?

 **How well can you read?**

In the case of more experienced readers, reading can be termed a somewhat simple process, as not every word is registered. Although this increases the speed of reading, it is easy to overlook mistakes, such as the additional "the" above, or to confuse similar-looking words. It becomes even more difficult when words and the background are non-distinguishable. Or were you able to make out the word "LIFE" (opposite page, top) right away?

Quickly go through the words on the opposite page one after the other. Ignore the meanings attributed to the words and say the color of the words out loud. Where do you get stuck?

When Green Reads Blue

The first two rows of this test can be read without a problem. However, as soon as the meaning and the respective color of the word no longer coincide, a higher level of concentration is required to keep the contradictory information apart. Saying colors out loud takes longer and mistakes become more frequent. In this case, you are experiencing the so-called Stroop effect, named after American psychologist John Ridley Stroop. It demonstrates how difficult it is to suppress the automatic process of trying to understand what we read even when we consciously try to ignore the meaning of the words. The Stroop effect is used in psychology to test a person's ability to focus.

red blue orange purple

orange blue green red

blue purple green red

orange blue red green

purple orange red blue

green red blue purple

orange red blue green

blue purple orange red

 In this picture, a couple of the coins are flying directly at you. To see them, hold the book in front of your face so that the tip of your nose touches the page. Stare straight ahead, as if you wanted to look through the picture, or squint. Once your eyes have lost all orientation, slowly move the picture away. If you are able to keep gazing into empty space (it isn't easy), the coins should jump out at you on their own.

3D Visions

Autostereograms, such as this coin image, consist of horizontally repeating patterns in which minor changes are built into the repetitions. In the above example, the background pattern varies throughout the image because the large coins have been slightly moved sideways, little by little. In addition to these minor sideway shifts, some of the large coins have also been turned almost imperceptibly. When you bring this picture very close to your face, your two eyes focus on different repetitions and therefore send slightly differing images to your brain, which then converts them into what appears to be a three-dimensional image. Don't be discouraged if you cannot see the flying riches in this picture. Many people need a lot of practice to develop their "magic eye"— while some never manage it at all.

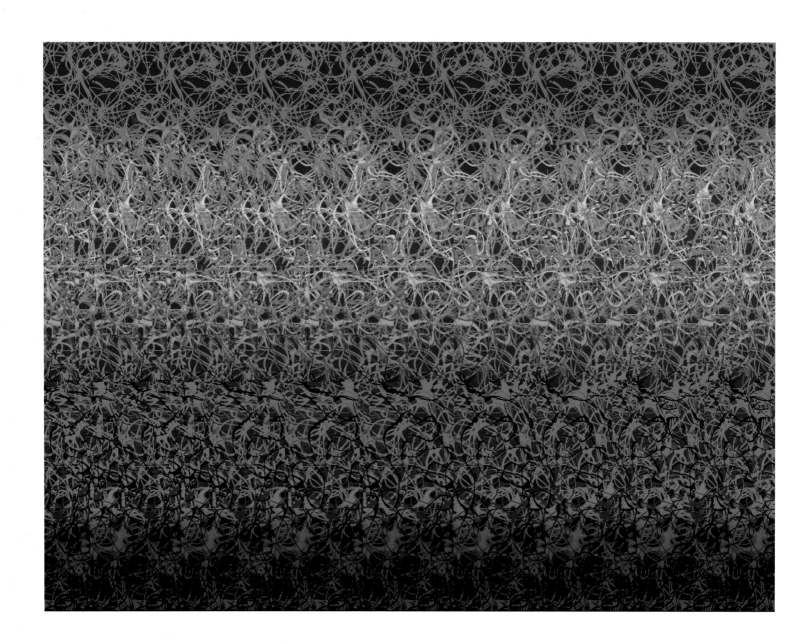

Look at these two autostereograms using the technique described on page 176. Discover the Happy New Year's message above and three-dimensional bubbles on the opposite page.

28.2 Are you able to look cross-eyed? If not, you won't be able to see the secret of the pictures shown here. Hold the book at arm's length and place the index finger of your free hand on the line between each double photo. Focus on the tip of your finger and slowly move your finger to your nose while maintaining your focus on the tip of your finger. With some practice, each pair of pictures should merge into one.

How does it work? By looking cross-eyed, the left eye focuses on a certain point in the right picture and the right eye on a point in the left picture. The pictures above were taken using a special camera with two lenses. Two pictures were taken of the same scene, one slightly shifted, which is how our eyes see. Normally, the brain reconstructs images of spatial depth from the minimal shifts in perspective. This also works by looking cross-eyed at a pair of two-dimensional pictures.

Can you see the hill? Now turn the book upside down.

What's Up, What's Down?

To most people, the image on the right appears to be a hill. However, it is actually a crater— the Barringer Crater in Arizona. It is the lighting that makes us see an elevation when the image is held the right way up, and an abyss when it is turned upside down. We are used to seeing light coming from above. The bright rim of the crater is therefore perceived as the slopes of a hill, and the dark rim as shadows inside the crater. Designers of graphic interfaces for computer programs use this effect to make buttons appear three-dimensional.

These two pictures look like reliefs (one protruding from the sand, the other pressed into it), don't they? Turn the book upside down to see how the images change.

30 Which part of the cube is facing the front, and which part is at the back?

Switching Sides

The Necker cube is an ambiguous image, or reversible figure, and is a particularly impressive example of bistable perception. The cube can only be perceived diagonally from above or diagonally from below, but never simultaneously. After a while, our perception of it will switch back and forth between the two, even if we try to focus on one viewpoint only.

   The cube was named after the Swiss geologist Louis Albert Necker, who discovered this effect while working on drawings of crystals in 1832.

Is the orange cube inside the blue cube or floating in front of it?

Many of the illusions in this book have already demonstrated that depth perception is based on subjective interpretation. Scientists have been studying this phenomenon for a long time. Early examples date back to 1899, when it was covered by the monthly magazine *Popular Science*. Look at the three rectangular blocks below and notice how your perception is constantly shifting according to whether your brain is trying to see an upper or lower view. It shows that a great deal in this world depends on perspective.

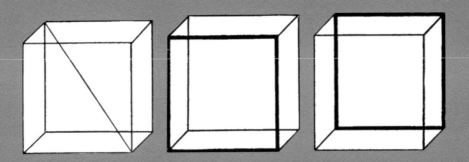

30.2 Piling up or hanging down?

This pattern actually works both ways. Most people will understand the image on the opposite page as a series of rectangular blocks stacked up on top of each other. This has to do with our visual experience, which tells us that objects are usually illuminated from above or from the side. Bright areas are therefore usually on top, which is why the patterns shown here always work for this effect, no matter from which side you look at them.

The Romans also discovered the fun side of playing with perception, as can be seen in the Roman mosaic above (also see page 106).

 **The moon appears to be much larger on the horizon than it does at its zenith — or does it?**

Natural Fakes

It may not look like it to us, but the size of the moon never changes, not even during the night when it rises from the horizon up into the sky. Just hold up your thumb at arm's length next to the moon and you will see that regardless of where the moon is, your thumb will always appear three to four times larger than the moon (depending on the length of your arm and the width of your thumb).

Why most people have this illusion is an ancient question, one that Aristotle, da Vinci, and Kepler were already trying to answer back in their day. The most plausible explanation for this phenomenon seems to be subjective or perceptual size constancy. Normally, our brain calculates the actual size of an object from the size perceived on the retina and calculates its distance. We often see the moon gleaming behind distant mountains and landmarks, which is why our brain assumes the moon to be far away and, accordingly, enlarges our perception of it. In its zenith in the night sky, however, the moon appears small, because the context needed by the brain to adjust the size is lacking.

31.1 Each of these mountain ridges appears to be darker at the top. Or is it deceiving us?

Actually, the luminosity of each mountain ridge is exactly the same from top to bottom. But where one ridge meets another, our perception increases the contrast. As a result, the darker ridge appears darker, and the lighter ridge lighter. In daily life, this increase in contrast helps us to perceive fine distinctions, usually attributed to lateral inhibition of the optic neuron cells in the eye. This is the case when the cells, stimulated by light, inhibit their immediate neighbors (see the explanation for the Hermann grid on page 8). However, higher levels of processing in the brain are probably also at play here. This effect was named the Chevreul illusion after the French chemist and color theorist who discovered it: Eugène Chevreul (1786–1889).

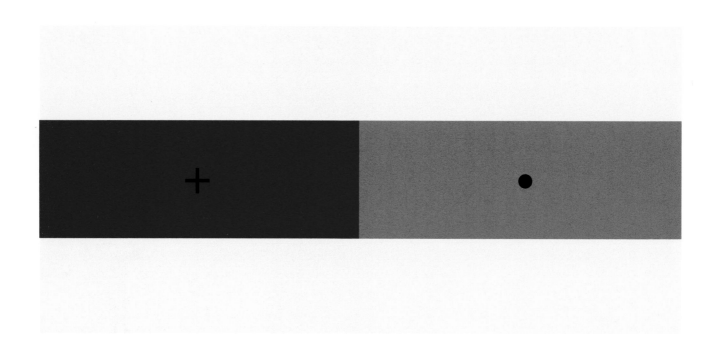

 Cover up your right eye and look at the black dot in the illustration above with your left eye. Play a little to find the right distance between your eye and the book so that you see the point at which the cross disappears.

Hokus-Pokus Disappearibus

The missing cross has, so to speak, become the victim of your blind spot. This is the place on the retina where the optical nerve is located. Since no receptor cells are located there, the eye is actually blind in this particular spot. Thanks to the cognitive process known as filling-in, we rarely notice this in our daily lives. As our example shows, the cross does not really disappear into a dark spot. Instead, the brain automatically fills in the gap with the immediate surrounding visual information, in this case, the color red.

You can experiment with a slightly different effect on the opposite page. This experiment was discovered in 1804 by I.P.V. Troxler and named after him. When the eye focuses on a particular point, an unchanging stimulus away from the fixation point will fade away and disappear. Stare at the black dot for at least 30 seconds and watch the colors vanish.

Focus on the center of this jumbled checkered pattern. Can you see how the irregularities are "ironed out"?

With his Healing Grid illusion, Ryota Kanai of University College London entered the finals of the Vision Sciences Society's 2005 "Illusion of the Year" contest. His illusion clearly shows how the brain irons out irregularities in its image of the world. It does so in order to adjust to its expectations and experience. Focus your eyes and your attention on the center of the grid. Can you see how the regularity in the pattern of the grid spreads to the periphery vision? The fact that there is actually a jumbled-up mess is gradually suppressed by our perception — at least until we focus our *fovea centralis* on it once again. As the area in our retina with the sharpest vision and also the center of our visual attention, the *fovea centralis* is not easily fooled.

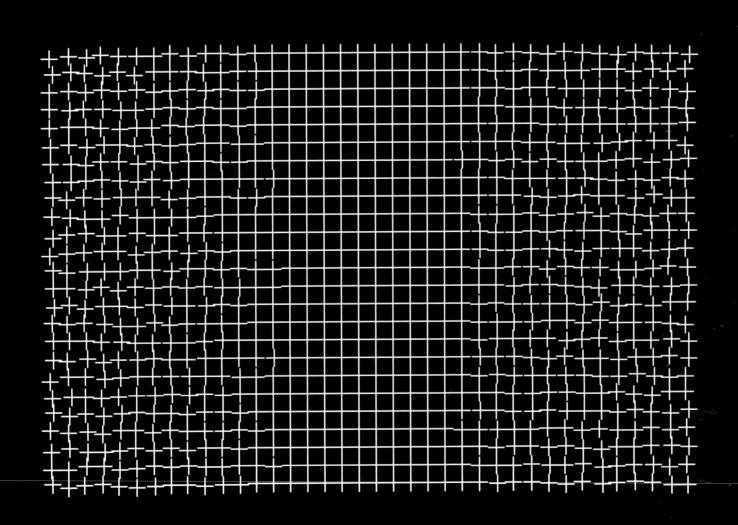

 **How many different shades of color can you make out in the image on the opposite page?**

In a Color Storm

Most people make out seven or eight colors. However, there are really only five: blue, yellow, red, green, and pink. The light and dark varieties of the last three colors are actually identical. The Munker-White illusion, which also works in black and white (the gray areas have the identical tone), has been confounding visual researchers for decades, as the red shape on the right should, according to the rules of contrast enhancement, appear darker. After all, the red areas are mainly surrounded by bright yellow. Nevertheless, the red on the right appears brighter than the red shape to its left, which is mostly surrounded by blue. Scientists call this effect "assimilation." It is still unclear if this contrast enhancement can be overcome. It most probably depends on the size of the colored shape. The effect decreases when the image is viewed close up.

Let your eyes wander over this image. Can you see the bright-colored grid with the vertically and horizontally aligned lines on a slightly beige background?

Once again, this effect is based on false perception. The red lines tint the background, which is actually white. Researchers have been unable to find a definite answer as to how the light-blue crosses at the intersections produce the luminous grid. This illusion, a version by Akiyoshi Kitaoka, works only when viewed from a certain distance. Viewed too closely, the beige haze disappears, and with it the checkered pattern.

 Look at all the illustrations individually. Are the colors of the shorter, vertical stripes similar? Are the colors of the two horizontal yellow stripes similar, or different?

Even if you cannot see it, you have probably guessed that the colors in each case are identical.

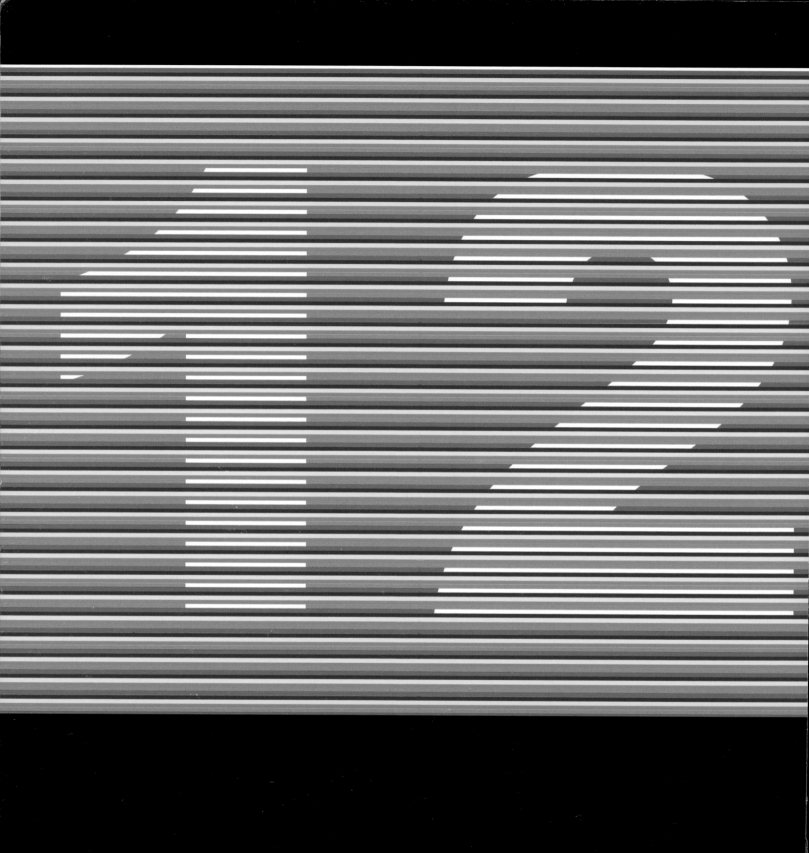

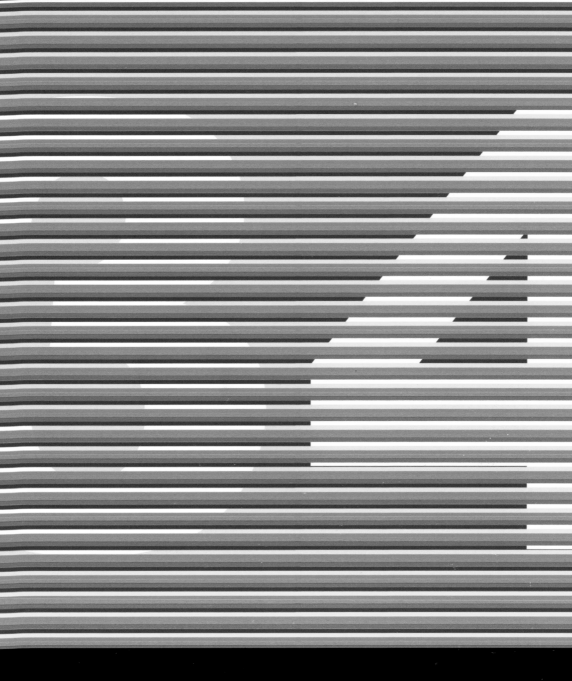

 What color(s) are the numbers?

All of the numbers are actually white, but the different-colored lines running through them trick our eyes.